D1213433

The Sword and the Cross

BY ROBERT M. GRANT

The Bible in the Church
The Sword and the Cross

The Sword and the Cross

by ROBERT M.ᶜ *Queen* GRANT

THE MACMILLAN COMPANY
NEW YORK 1955

Copyright, 1955, by The Macmillan Company

All rights reserved—no part of this book may be reproduced in any form without permission in writing from the publisher, except by a reviewer who wishes to quote brief passages in connection with a review written for inclusion in magazine or newspaper.

PRINTED IN THE UNITED STATES OF AMERICA

FIRST PRINTING

Let every person be subject to the governing authorities. For there is no authority except from God, and those that exist have been instituted by God. Therefore he who resists the authorities resists what God has appointed, and those who resist will incur judgment. For rulers are not a terror to good conduct, but to bad. Would you have no fear of him who is in authority? Then do what is good, and you will receive his approval, for he is God's servant for your good. But if you do wrong, be afraid, for he does not bear the sword in vain; he is the servant of God to execute his wrath on the wrong-doer. Therefore one must be subject, not only to avoid God's wrath but also for the sake of conscience.

Romans 13, 1-5 (REVISED STANDARD VERSION)

*If anyone is to be taken captive,
    to captivity he goes;
if anyone slays with the sword,
    with the sword shall he be slain.*

Revelation 13, 10 (REVISED STANDARD VERSION)

Contents

I. THE REPUBLIC

1 Rome and Religion

WHY DID THE ROMAN GOVERNMENT PERSECUTE CHRISTIANITY AND OTHER foreign religions? Why did it persecute them intermittently rather than constantly? To answer these questions we must go back more than two thousand years, to the time when Rome was achieving control of the Mediterranean world. We must look at one of the most dramatic stories to come out of ancient times—a drama whose implications for our own world will be plain to everyone concerned with politics or religion.

The characters of the story include nearly every important person in antiquity. There are gods and goddesses, men and women, emperors and slaves, philosophers and priests. There are murdered men who became gods and self-deified men who were murdered. There are the Roman senators who destroyed temples and killed worshipers and then rebuilt the temples. Among the actors are the mad Caligula and the benign Antoninus Pius. There are martyrs, near martyrs, and those who discreetly avoided martyrdom.

The state is the civilized world of their time. The action covers a period of five hundred years. It begins when Rome was a small but powerful republic. It ends with the final toleration of the Christians. In the interval we trace Rome's suppression of alien religions, and its losing battle to remain purely Roman.

To begin our story we must first recognize the close relation of Roman religion to the Roman state. We must understand the Roman tradition of suppressing religions when they were regarded as un-Roman and subversive to moral or political order. We must consider

9

the rise of Oriental religions at the end of the republic, since Christianity was not the only religion attacked by the Roman state.

We must also bear in mind the relation of these Oriental religions to the class warfare which developed in the last century before Christ and contributed much to the destruction of the republic. On one side stood the Roman Senate and the traditional Roman religion which served the state. On the other stood many of the Roman people, whose religious needs could not be satisfied by the outworn traditional forms. Out of this conflict developed some of the legal precedents which were later to guide the state in its dealings with the Christian problem.

The Roman republic and empire were not unique in antiquity because their religion was official. Most priesthoods were state priesthoods. The priests had no special character except that derived from their relation to the state. The strangeness of Roman religion lay in its gods and rites. The gods the Romans served were in part old Etruscan gods taken over by the Romans, in part abstractions developed by the Romans out of earlier, more specific, worships, and in part Greek gods gradually introduced into the Roman circle.

In Roman religion the gods were ultimately not so important as the rites with which they were worshiped. These rites had to be performed with the most minute precision; if a Roman pontiff made a mistake he had to go back and repeat a whole ceremony over from the beginning.

Associated with the worship of the gods was an elaborate system of prediction of the future, derived finally from the Etruscans, and based largely on the examination of various natural phenomena such as the flight of birds and the spots on an animal's liver. Through investigation of these phenomena the augurs were able to predict the future of the Roman state with some precision. Rome, the state, and Roman religion were inextricably bound together.

The greatest of the gods were Jupiter, the god of thunder and the Roman state, and his wife Juno. Originally no mythology was associated with them, but the Romans borrowed Greek mythology concerning Zeus and Hera. Eventually Jupiter was identified with Zeus, and all the philosophical speculation associated with Zeus clustered around Jupiter.

According to legend the city of Rome was related to Greek mythology, for the Trojan prince Aeneas, fleeing from burning Troy, finally settled in Latium, and at a later date (to be precise, 753 B.C.) a certain Romulus founded the city of Rome. By reading ancient history in the light of their own times, the Romans decided that Romulus had been assassinated by a group opposed to one-man rule, but that for the sake of popular support this group had claimed that Romulus had ascended into heaven. There with the other gods his divinity was acknowledged and he ruled for ever and ever. His deification was ultimately to provide a precedent for the deification of Julius Caesar and the Roman emperors who followed him.

It must be admitted, however, that for the lower classes the official Roman religion was bare and unimpressive. Only the power of the state could commend it to them. They constantly strove to find religions with more emotional content, more promise for the future, than the simple (should we say Puritanical?) old Roman religion. To them the correct performance of traditional rites came to be meaningless. To them, as their interests came to be distinct from the interests of the aristocracy, Jupiter and Juno occupied an exalted position remote from their own situation. Therefore the history of Roman religion is the history of incessant popular pressure brought upon the aristocracy which adhered to the old ways. Among the people there was always an interest in the more emotionally satisfying Greek and Oriental worships in which it was plain that the gods took a personal interest in the affairs of believers.

The pressure for such worships grew gradually more intense, especially during the first century B.C., when Cicero, an augur himself, hints that augurs might wink skeptically at one another as they went through the ceremonies. If there was anything which the people could not tolerate, it was being hoodwinked in the name of the gods. Under such circumstances Greek and Oriental religions flourished to an amazing extent, and their flourishing did not end with the end of the republic but continued throughout the life of the empire. When the cult of the emperor developed, there were many (not only Jews and Christians) who suspected the motives of the Roman Senate and the old Roman nobility. The Roman world was waiting for something new.

Our first concern is to examine the difficulties faced by the Roman government when it confronted foreign religions. Every state is a system of power resting not only on force but also on an ideology. Romans held that their power could be attributed to the gods of Rome. The gods of other nations had demonstrated their inferiority to the Roman gods by failing to protect these nations against the power of Rome's legions. Therefore other peoples living in Italy now owed allegiance to the Roman gods, not to the gods of Greece or the Orient, and those who introduced the worship of foreign divinities were inevitably suspected of subversive activity. At times of crisis the Senate might vote to introduce the worship of some foreign deity to Rome, but such introductions were carefully regulated and controlled. These gods became Roman gods. Thus the black stone of the Mother of the Gods was brought from Pessinus to Rome; she became the Roman Mother.

On the other hand, when immigrants, sometimes prisoners of war, brought their deities with them no such supervision was possible. Livy gives a vivid description of the Bacchic rites introduced to Etruria by an ill-born Greek. It is difficult to determine what Livy's account owes to his own imagination and what comes from the reports of the investigation made by the consul, but an inscription proves that the penalties described by Livy were actually decreed. The cult was wild and un-Roman; initiates took an oath not to reveal the mysteries to anyone, and men joined with women in wailing to the accompaniment of cymbals and tambourines. The men jumped about frantically and uttered ecstatic words of "prophecy."

Two considerations are mentioned as especially influential in the suppression of these rites. One is the moral problem: The Bacchants were supposed to have taken an oath binding them to the performance of every kind of crime, perhaps including cannibalism. In his speech the consul states that "among them the essence of religion is to consider nothing as immoral." The other consideration is the political and administrative problem: secret nocturnal meetings were in themselves suspect, and those of the Bacchants might lead to setting fire to the city.

The character of the principal witness to these rites and beliefs was not above reproach. She was a prostitute named Hispala, who had formerly participated in the rites but had abandoned them. But the consul had discovered that "a great multitude, nearly another people," was participating, and their participation could not be tolerated. The number of those involved was found to be more than seven thousand, and of these more than half were executed. For the future, the religion was tolerated, but no more than five persons (two men, three women) were to meet at once, and they had to obtain a license from the city praetor.

Foreign religions were often considered, then, as threats to the morality and the very existence of the state and its own official religion.

At a later date there were repeated difficulties over the worship of the Egyptian deities Isis and Serapis. In 58 B.C., the consul Gabinius took cognizance of a decree of the Senate, in spite of popular enthusiasm for the Egyptian gods, and refused to allow altars set up on the Capitol. Various decrees later condemned private or public shrines. The official attitude was related to hostility against the Egypt of Cleopatra and Antony. And although in 43 B.C. the triumvirs actually decreed the building of a temple of Isis, Augustus did not permit Egyptian cults inside the *pomerium*, the sacred area of the old city of Rome. In A.D. 19 a scandal at a temple near the Tiber resulted in official intervention and another attempt at suppression.

This Roman policy is set forth not only in Livy's description of the Bacchanalia but also in the advice which Dio Cassius describes Maecenas as giving Augustus. The worship of the Roman gods is to be maintained, and new and foreign divinities are to be rejected. "Hate and punish those who introduce foreign gods." Such punishment is necessary not only for the sake of the Roman gods, who surely do not want others preferred before them, but also for the sake of the principate, for from foreign religions conspiracies arise. This was in fact Augustus' attitude: he despised most foreign religions.

Thus he forbade the participation of Roman citizens in the rites of the Druids of Gaul and Britain. Again the reasons are related to morality and security. The Druids were not only politically dangerous but also inhumanly barbarous; human sacrifice was carried on in their rites. Claudius, who found even a Roman knight carrying a magic egg of the Druids, totally abolished their religion within the empire. The Druids reciprocated this dislike. When the temple of Jupiter Capitolinus was burned in the year 69, they held that the fire was a sign of heavenly wrath and that the empire would pass to the nations beyond the Alps.

Again, under Tiberius the conspiracy of Libo Drusus was encouraged by Chaldaean astrologers. Therefore a decree of the Senate in the year 16 expelled them from Italy, while two of them were put to death. According to Suetonius, those who recanted and promised to abandon the art were pardoned. Under Nero in the year 52 a Roman patrician was exiled on the ground that he had asked Chaldaeans about the death of the emperor, and a new and severe decree of the Senate once more expelled astrologers. Its failure is illustrated by the fact that it was repeated under Vitellius in the year 69.

The Jewish religion was a special case. Nationalism and religion were more closely related in the case of the Jews than in that of any other people, and Roman writers never tire of remarking on the exclusiveness and misanthropy of the Jews. Already in the year 139 a *praetor peregrinus* expelled astrologers from Rome and also those persons who were thought to be introducing the worship of Jupiter Sabazius. Modern critics have sometimes thought that these were syncretistic-minded Hellenistic Jews, but we shall try to show that this notion is wrong. Under the early emperors Jews were exempted from military service and from the imperial cult (except for a time under Caligula), and most procurators of Judaea respected Jewish religious customs. Claudius explicitly restored the privileges lost under Caligula.

Occasionally action was taken against the Jews under special circumstances. In Tiberius' time a decree of the Senate enrolled four thousand Jewish freedmen in the army and sent them to Sardinia, while other Jews were expelled from Italy "unless before a certain

day they abandoned their profane rites." According to Suetonius
the decree was applied to proselytes as well, and provided perpetual
slavery as the alternative to exile or recantation. A similar edict was
issued by Claudius, perhaps toward the middle of his reign. At the
end of the first Jewish war various Jews were accused of conspiracy,
but according to Josephus his own influence over Vespasian resulted
in their acquittal.

In times of crisis and Jewish rebellion, the association of early
Christianity with Judaism could hardly improve the Christians' position in the Roman eyes. We have already seen that the Druids were
put down largely because of their practice of human sacrifice; the
same charge was made against the Jews, and later against Christians.
The Christians inherited the odium attached to other foreign religions, as well as that derived from Jewish nationalism. They preached
the imminent reign of God, and were inevitably suspected of forming a conspiracy to bring it into existence. Romans often thought
that such conspiracies were bound together by oaths sealed in human
blood. This was probably the case in the affair of the Bacchanalia
and was certainly a fact in the Catilinarian conspiracy toward the end
of the republic. The Christian covenant ratified in the blood of Jesus
could hardly fail to be misunderstood as similar. If we remember that
the Christians went out into the world with the gospel of the second
coming of Jesus and the rite of the Lord's Supper, we cannot be
surprised at Roman suspicion and hatred.

But what precisely was the attitude of the Roman state toward the
adherents of this new religion? The author of Luke-Acts tries to
show his readers that Roman authorities were consistently favorable
toward Christians, and that only Jewish malice was responsible for
their troubles. Other historians do not give this impression, and it
seems likely that Christians were treated like adherents of other dangerous foreign cults. This conclusion has recently been expressed by
Professor Nock.

When *Isiaci* and Jews were banished from Rome under Tiberius no question arose whether this or that individual had committed any offence save
that of being what he was; when astrologers were expelled, it was all who
were identified as such and not only those who had answered questions

about the ruler's horoscope. When Druidical cultus was put down, all its practices were suppressed, not simply human sacrifice or magic. So from Trajan's time, at least, to profess Christianity and to act as Christians did was in itself enough to make a man liable to the death penalty.

We must add one point to this statement, since it is so significant for Roman dealings with Christians. The astrologers and Jews expelled by Tiberius were indeed punished simply as astrologers and as Jews, but explicit mention is made of the possibility of recantation. One who promised that he would no longer practice astrology or the rites of Judaism did not suffer the penalty and apparently received a full pardon. In the case of the Bacchanalia and of Druid worship no such pardon was possible, and we must assume that this severity (as Cicero calls it in the case of the Bacchanalia) was due to the shocking nature of the cultus. The fact that Christians were almost invariably asked to recant suggests that Roman officials did not believe the rumors about their immorality.

The Christians were thus punished because their religion was believed to be inimical to the interests of the state. This belief was shared by the people and the rulers alike, but only in times of crisis did it become a belief which required aggressive action. Ordinarily Christians were regarded as potentially but not actually dangerous to the peace and security of the Roman empire.

2 Strange Gods

ROMAN OFFICIAL RELIGION REPRESENTS A STRANGE COMBINATION OF hostility toward foreign cults with sporadic acceptance of them, usually for political motives. A temple had been built to Apollo as early as 433 B.C. Other Greek gods had also been admitted, though not within the *pomerium*. And after the passage of the Ogulnian Law in 300, which admitted plebeians to the highest priesthoods, the Greek god Asclepius was introduced from Epidaurus along with Greek cultus. This god was a god of healing, and during an epidemic in the year 293 the Sibylline Books revealed that he should be brought to the city. Because a war was being waged, it was impossible to do more than have a day of prayer to Asclepius that year, but two years later an embassy was sent to Epidaurus. It was headed by Q. Ogulnius, who with his brother had been responsible for the Ogulnian Law. From Epidaurus the ambassadors brought a sacred snake, which they placed in a temple built on the island in the Tiber (outside the *pomerium*). The island remained sacred to Asclepius in late imperial times. Unlike earlier foreign cults brought to Rome, that of Asclepius remained foreign. Wissowa points out that "as in Epidaurus, snakes and dogs were kept there, the sick were brought in, received through incubation the necessary information for their treatment, and after being healed dedicated inscriptions of gratitude and votive offerings to the god." The introduction of Asclepius was presumably due to popular pressure.

Other Greek gods followed, but the climax of infiltration was reached in the chaos of the second Carthaginian war. In 218-217 B.C. the Carthaginian general Hannibal was in northern Italy, and as Livy says, men's minds were "moved toward religion." During early 217 miraculous phenomena were reported at first in Rome and Italy, then (as Hannibal moved southward) in Sicily and Sardinia. The Senate decided that it was necessary to provide official recognition of the religious situation, and ordered a great *lectisternium*, in which twenty-four deities reclined on cushions. Twelve of these gods and goddesses were Greek, twelve Roman. Here we see a genuine crisis-theology; the religious needs of the Roman people could not be satisfied by Roman religion alone, and it was necessary to turn to the East.

In the following four years there were recurrent waves of religious enthusiasm; Hannibal had been defeated but his army remained in Italy. Eighty thousand Romans had been killed at Cannae. In 213 there was so much religious excitement that not only privately but also publicly, even in the Forum and on the Capitol, a mob of women sacrificed and prayed to the gods. These women rejected the old Roman cults in favor of foreign deities and foreign rites. Under these circumstances the praetor issued an edict that everyone who

possessed private forms of prophecy (as contrasted with the Sibylline Books) or prayer or rules of sacrifice should bring them to him
before the Kalends of April, and that no one should sacrifice publicly
with any strange or foreign rite. This mild edict produced the desired effect, and the religious revival gradually came to an end. In
212 B.C. the praetor made public an oracle which (he said) he had
received; it correctly predicted the battle of Cannae, which had occurred five years earlier, and ordered the institution of religious
games for Apollo.

The religious problem remained difficult, especially around 205,
when Hannibal was once more in Italy. In that year an unusual hail-
storm was taken as the occasion for consulting the Sibylline Books,
which, perhaps with some concern for Roman allies in Asia Minor,
announced that Hannibal would leave Italy if the Great Mother of
the Gods were brought from Phrygia to the temple of Victory on
the Palatine. In 204 the Great Mother was brought to Rome; her arrival on April 4 was celebrated by a *lectisternium* (the other gods
greeting their mother?) and the establishment of an official festival.
The Great Mother was the first Oriental deity to be accepted at
Rome, and she was introduced by an embassy which included five
of the leading members of the Roman nobility. When she reached
Rome (in the form of a meteorite) she was met, according to the
legend, by the noble matron Claudia Quinta. Nothing could show
better the desire of the aristocracy to provide national unity on the
basis of religion, a religion introduced by the aristocracy and controlled by the aristocracy. No Roman citizen, however, was allowed
to take part in her wild Phrygian rites, performed by Phrygian
priests; for Romans there were the more sedate Megalensia (the festival day) and the Ludi Megalenses.

The prophecy of the Sibyl was fulfilled in the year 202, when the
war came to an end. Eight years later, just before a war with Antiochus III in Greece, the Ludi were first performed in dramatic form.
In 191 the temple of the Great Mother was dedicated on the Palatine.
The next year Antiochus was decisively defeated. Thus her position
was secure. Both her temporary quarters in the temple of Victory
and her permanent residence were on the Palatine, within the *po-*

merium. An Oriental religion had won admission to the heart of the Roman state. When the temple burned in A.D. 3, it was Augustus who rebuilt it. Roman citizens, however, do not seem to have been priests of the Phrygian cult until the end of the second century.

Four years after the defeat of Antiochus, it became evident that Roman domestic problems required attention. The Great Mother had become more or less Roman, under aristocratic auspices. Adherents of other foreign cults apparently thought that their gods too could flourish in Rome and Italy, without benefit of senatorial favor. In 186 B.C. the attention of the praetor was brought to the unauthorized rites of the Bacchanalia. This famous case, involving a scandal which offended Roman morality, provided a precedent for all later dealings with foreign religions.

The Bacchanalian rites had long been celebrated by women in a sacred grove near the Aventine, but only on three days during the year. Now, however, a priestess from South Italy, under Greek influence, initiated men into the cult and held meetings weekly. Under the stimulus of common food and drink, wild sexual orgies took place and led to murders (perhaps with cannibalism), the forging of wills, and oaths of disloyalty to the state. When information about these meetings reached the consul, Spurius Postumius Albinus, he asked the Senate for authority to conduct a thorough investigation in order to suppress the cult. A panic resulted, since about seven thousand men and women were involved. Their leaders were, as might be expected, prominent plebeians. All were arrested, though a distinction was made between those who had merely been initiated and those who had acted on the criminal oath they had taken. The first group was sentenced to life imprisonment, while the second was given capital punishment. According to Livy the second group was larger than the first. This action was followed by a second decree of the Senate. This decree absolutely forbade the Bacchanalian assemblies; there were to be no common funds, no master of the rites, and no priest. An exception was made to the rule, however, presumably because of popular pressure. If an individual regarded the rites as essential, he could apply for permission to the urban praetor, who had to consult the Senate at a time when no fewer than one hundred senators were present. If permission was granted by the Senate, no more than five persons could be present at the rite.

This decree was sent by the consuls to the federated communities of Italy, and a bronze copy from South Italy is still in existence. The search for Bacchants continued in South Italy, where we hear of further arrests and executions in 184, 182, and 181. These repressive actions seem to have been effective. No trace of Bacchanalia is found in Italy until the second century of the empire, when an inscription proves that they had become respectable.

The suppression of the Bacchanalia provided the classical example for later dealings with foreign religions not accepted by the state. Livy himself ascribes a speech to the consul in which this suppression is related to the confiscation of foreign religious documents in 213 B.C. and is treated as the continuation of the policy of forbidding foreign rites. The consul's speech seems to reflect the policy of Augustus as much as that of the earlier consuls, but it must be remembered that this policy was in fact that of the Roman aristocracy for many centuries. Livy may not be giving a purely imaginative account.

When Cicero, nearly a century and a half later, deals with foreign religions and nocturnal rites in his treatise *On the Laws*, he gives the case of the Bacchanalia as the classical example of the Roman attitude. The language of Livy's account seems to be echoed in two later documents dealing with the Christians: Pliny's letter to the emperor Trajan and Fronto's oration against the Christians. To the Romans foreign religion, immorality, and conspiracy were closely associated.

In the years after 186 the problem of foreigners living in Rome and getting their names on the voting lists came to a crisis. Expulsions of Latins took place in 177 and 168, and a new difficulty in 161 was met with a decree of the Senate. After the victories of Roman troops in the East and Rome's attempts to provide freedom for Greece, Greek teachers of philosophy and rhetoric flocked to Rome, much to the dismay of sterner Romans such as the conservative Porcius Cato. Doubtless he was influential in the passage of a decree which instructed the urban praetor to expel philosophers and rhet-oricians.

In the same year the Senate expressed its friendship toward the new Jewish buffer state, for whose creation Rome had been partly responsible.

Five years later an Athenian embassy visited Rome, and its most prominent, or perhaps its most vocal, member was asked to give two lectures. This was the Academic philosopher Carneades. In his first lecture he proved conclusively that there was an absolute justice on which the power of the state rested. The next day, however, he proved equally conclusively that such justice did not exist. The ef-fect of these lectures on his audience was immediate. Cato, who had been present, asked that the decree of 161 be enforced against the embassy, but in view of the sanctity of ambassadors his wish could not be granted. In the following year, however, the praetor seems to have been able to find two other philosophers at Rome who could be expelled.

The following decade was marked by religious quiet at Rome, punctuated only by the erection of a few temples. In 142 a Jewish em-bassy visited the city in order to secure recognition for the high priest Simon, who had nearly secured complete control of his coun-try. The consul L. Metellus Calvus agreed and sent a circular letter to Rome's Eastern allies (with a copy to Simon), instructing them to return refugees to Simon for punishment in accordance with Jew-ish law. Two years later an embassy left Rome for a tour of inspec-tion throughout the East. Its members included the famous general Scipio Aemilianus, who had destroyed Carthage in 146, the ex-con-sul Metellus Calvus, and an official well acquainted with Greek lit-erature and Stoic philosophy, Spurius Mummius. Scipio took with him his friend the Stoic philosopher Panaetius. On its tour the em-bassy visited Alexandria and Syria, perhaps traveling as far as Baby-lon; then it returned through Pergamum and Athens to Rome, prob-ably in 139.

Therefore it is significant that in this year the "Chaldaeans" (as-trologers) were expelled from Rome and Italy, for Panaetius, as far as we know, was the only Stoic philosopher who strongly opposed astrology. During the journeys of the embassy he must have been able to express his disapproval to Scipio and the others, and to back it up with instances taken from observation. Perhaps it was on this journey that Panaetius observed that Scylax of Halicarnassus, a ruler who excelled in astronomy, entirely rejected the "Chaldaean" method of prediction. In any event, it seems significant that upon the embassy's return the astrologers were expelled because they received money on false pretences.

In the same year, according to Valerius Maximus, the praetor in charge of foreigners "compelled the Jews, who had tried to infect Roman ways with the cult of Jupiter Sabazius, to return to their homes." The picture of Judaism provided by this sentence is a singular one, and a great deal of imagination has been devoted to it by modern scholars. It is of course possible that Jewish refugees, perhaps from Asia Minor, were actually worshiping Zeus Sabazius, or that by confusing Yahweh Sabaoth with some form (not nominative) of the name Jupiter Sabazius the Roman police made a mistake. Alternatively, we may suggest that there is some confusion in the text, which is known to us only through two late epitomes. Two items seem to be combined. In the first place, the return of Jews to their homes seems to reflect the letter of Metellus Calvus about refugees; and since he visited Syria with the embassy, it may also reflect a request made personally to him by the high priest Simon. If refugees were to be returned by Rome's allies, why not by Rome? In the second place, the mention of Jupiter Sabazius may well reflect the embassy's visit to Pergamum and Athens. At Pergamum they must have seen the new shrine of Zeus Sabazius, erected in 142-141 because of the influence of the Cappadocian queen of Pergamum. At Athens they could learn that the most prominent foreign religion suppressed there was that of Sabazius, and surely a religion suppressed even in Greece could not be tolerated at Rome. Enthusiasts for Sabazius could be expelled to Pergamum.

If our analysis is correct (it requires only reading IUDAEO-SETEOSQUI for IUDAEOSQUI in Valerius Maximus), in 139 B.C. we find the Roman state expelling astrologers and worshipers of Zeus Sabazius. The case of the Jews was different; it involved only the return of refugees to their native land. The only expulsions of Jews from Rome, as we shall later see, took place under Tiberius and Claudius.

In the late second century B.C. Roman religion itself was influenced by party politics in the city, when human sacrifice was forbidden. In 114 a death by lightning was explained by the "prophets" (augurs) as due to the disgrace of the Vestals. A slave confirmed the augurs' suspicions by accusing three of the six Vestal virgins of adultery. The three bore the prominent names Aemilia, Licinia, and Marcia. The slave also accused his master, a man of equestrian rank. The Vestals were found guilty, and at the same time two Greeks and two Celts were buried alive, in accordance with ancient tradition. The event was momentarily forgotten in the ensuing foreign and domestic conflicts, but in 97 B.C., when a brief conservative reaction had returned the *optimates* to office, a decree of the Senate was passed which forbade human sacrifice. One of the consuls of that year was P. Licinius Crassus, second cousin of the Vestal Licinia. The decree was first enforced in Spain, to which Licinius went in 95. As Plutarch says, relying on Posidonius or the geographer Artemidorus of Ephesus, "when they heard that the barbarous tribe called the Bletonesii had sacrificed a man to their gods, they sent for their chiefs, intending to punish them; but on learning that they had done it in obedience to some custom, they set them free but forbade the practice for the future."

This decree has considerable importance in the relations between the Roman state and those religions which either practiced or were said to practice human sacrifice. We shall soon see the horror with which Romans greeted the discovery of human flesh in the secret shrine of Ma-Bellona; we shall encounter it again in Roman dealings with Druids and Christians.

Around the same time, during the crucial war with the Teutons and Cimbri, the dictator Marius was criticized for accepting guidance from a Syrian prophetess named Martha. The Senate had earlier rejected her offer of predictions, and she had managed to reach Marius through his wife, whom she convinced by correctly predicting which of two gladiators would be victorious. Marius was accustomed to offer sacrifices in accordance with Martha's decisions, although there were those, probably including his opponent Sulla, who suspected him of hypocrisy.

Just before Marius' great victory at Aquae Sextiae in 102, the priest of the Great Mother at Pessinus (jealous, perhaps, of Martha's influence) realized that it would be well to come to Rome and announce the Mother's promise of triumph for the Roman forces. The Senate responded by voting the erection of another temple for the Mother. Overcome with gratitude, the eager priest proposed to announce the news himself to the people, but a suspicious tribune of the people named Aulus Pompeius insultingly drove him from the rostrum, addressing him as a simple mendicant for the Mother. The news became known, however, and its accuracy was confirmed by the fact that Pompeius barely reached home before he was stricken with a high fever which resulted in his death within a week.

No record of the building of such a temple has survived, but we know that after the victory Marius erected a temple to the old Roman deities Honor and Virtue. He may also have made a pilgrimage to Pessinus in order to conform to the people's wishes, or to explain why the temple was not built, but the evidence is unclear.

In Roman political life by the early years of the first century B.C. it became genuinely necessary for those who desired the people's support to reverence the people's gods as well as those of the Senate. In Sulla's time the Egyptian religion came to Rome, and Sulla himself is our authority for the story that the Cappadocian goddess Ma-Bellona appeared to him as he was marching against the city.

3 Isis and the Class Struggle

IN THE AUTUMN OF THE YEAR 43 B.C., A CERTAIN MARCUS VOLUSIUS learned that his name was on the list of those marked for death by the three men who had seized power after the murder of Julius Caesar. He was an aedile of the people; that is to say, he was in charge of the cult of Ceres and had oversight of foreign religions at Rome.

During the year in which he was an aedile, he had seen the triumvirs yield to popular pressure and push through the Senate a decree providing for the erection of temples to the Egyptian deities Serapis and Isis, long forbidden in Rome. He himself was on good terms with a priest of Isis. Now the festival of Isis, a pageant of Isis' recovery of the body of her dead divine husband Osiris, was under way, and crowds were thronging to watch it. The god Anubis, too, took part in the pageant, wearing his jackal's head and helping Isis in her search for Osiris. The proscribed aedile had to escape from Rome, and fortunately the priest of Isis was willing to let him wear the long linen costume of the Isiacs as well as the jackal's head of Anubis. In this garb Volusius escaped through the crowds and made his way to Sicily.

Valerius Maximus, relating the event seventy-five years later, in the reign of an emperor opposed to non-Roman religions, comments on it thus: "What is more miserable than the necessity which forced a magistrate of the Roman people, without his insignia of office, to go through the city concealed by the emblems of a foreign religion?"

In the escape of Volusius we see a symbol of the whole struggle of the Roman state, and especially of the Roman aristocracy, to preserve its native religion against the un-Roman influences pressing from abroad. We see the triumph of the people to whom the Egyptian religion was more meaningful that the old Roman religion; we see the part politics always played in the religious problem, and the part religion always played in politics. In the comment of Valerius Maximus we see the attitude of the Roman aristocracy which could not tolerate religions unless and until these religions served the purposes of the state.

The religion of Egypt had long been making progress in Italy. Like other Oriental religions, it had apparently first entered Italy through the port of Puteoli near Naples; thence it had spread to Pompeii, where remains of a temple have been found which go back to the second century B.C. In the time of the superstitious popular leader Sulla it had entered Rome itself, and before the middle of the first century B.C. there was a temple of Isis on the Capitoline hill.

In the struggles between the Roman aristocracy and the people which led to civil wars, the Egyptian cults played a prominent role. They were popular, and they came to be regarded as symbols of the people's interests. From Pompeian wall scribbling we know that the Isiacs, the worshipers of Isis, were active in politics.

The Roman aristocracy was firmly opposed to Egyptian religion, and firmly attached to the ancient Roman cult. Late in the year 59 the Senate took action against the popular Egyptian religion, and decreed that the altars of the Egyptian gods Serapis and Isis should be removed from the Capitol. They were removed. On the first day of the following year the new consul Gabinius, elected by "popular" support, could hardly inspect the animals sacrificed at his inauguration because of the crowd of members of the "popular" party who complained that he had made no decision about Serapis and Isis. Shortly thereafter he decided to obey the Senate rather than the people. He prohibited the erection of new altars, perhaps because he was leaving the popular party in favor of the triumvirs, who had promised him that he would be governor of a wealthy province. The Senate was able to enforce this regulation, and a temple of Isis did not appear on the Capitol until many years later.

The conflict of parties continued, however, and in 53 B.C., when Pompey held supreme power with backing from the aristocracy (the *optimates*), no consuls were elected until the month of July. After their election and the convening of the Senate, it was decreed that private shrines of Serapis and Isis should be destroyed, "since the Senate did not regard these gods with favor." A series of unfavorable omens followed in January of the next year, but it was hard to tell their exact meaning. Presumably the *populares* took them one way and the *optimates* another.

In 50 B.C. one of the consuls was the patrician L. Aemilius Paulus. Member of an ancient and honorable family, he had been an aedile five years earlier, and had begun to restore the Basilica Aemilia, built more than a century before when a member of his family was censor. When he was elected with senatorial support against the triumvirs, one of his acts was to enforce the previous decrees of the Senate against Egyptian temples, which had obviously been erected during Pompey's brief dictatorship at Rome. Unfortunately, he was unable

to find a workman who would touch the sacred building; he therefore laid aside his toga, took the ax, and fixed it in the temple's doors,
His usefulness to the conservative party soon ended. Shortly there-
after, Caesar enabled him to continue his restoration of the family
basilica by a bribe of 1500 talents (about two million dollars), and
he retired from political activity. The Egyptian temples, however,
were not at once rebuilt.

Two years later, after Caesar had become consul, and Pompey had
been murdered, and Caesar had sailed for Alexandria after being
made dictator, a surprising omen took place on the Capitol. In spite
of the advent of winter, a swarm of bees was observed about the
statue of Hercules. Such an omen was generally regarded as unfavorable, and the college of augurs had to be convened to discover what
it meant. Their decision was duly rendered: in their opinion the
nearby precincts of Serapis and Isis, where the temple of Isis had
once stood, ought to be razed to the ground. This action was performed, and the wreckers came upon a hidden temple of the Cappadocian goddess Ma-Bellona. In it were pots full of human flesh—or
so Dio Cassius says. A series of frightful prodigies immediately followed, which the augurs rightly interpreted as portents of further
class warfare.

After Caesar's murder and the seizure of uncertain power by the
new triumvirate, the Senate found it necessary to conciliate the people by providing for the reconstruction of the Egyptian temples.
The Senate returned to its old attitude once Marcus Antonius became embroiled with Cleopatra VII, queen of Egypt. In 34 B.C. he
appeared as Dionysus at a festival in Alexandria in which the queen,
who called herself "the new Isis," appeared as the Egyptian goddess.
When Octavian broke with Antonius, and overwhelmed his fleet
at Actium in 31, he viewed Egypt and Egyptian religion with traditional suspicion. On his return to Rome in 28, he dedicated the new
temple of Apollo on the Palatine and forbade the erection of Egyptian temples within the *pomerium*, the city of Rome as defined by
the augurs. A few years later Vitruvius tells us that there were such
temples in the market place by the Tiber.

The policy of Octavian is presented in summary and idealized form, and ascribed to Maecenas, by Dio Cassius. It required adherence to the ancestral rites and firm rejection of foreign religions, partly on the ground that they led to alien customs which in turn led to conspiracies. In any case, this policy was followed. In 21, when Agrippa was temporarily representing Octavian in Rome, he excluded Egyptian temples from the suburbs as well. Octavian's views are described by Suetonius as combining reverence for old foreign religions favored at Rome, such as the respectable mysteries of Eleusis, with contempt for others, such as the Egyptian and the Jewish cults.

We hear nothing further about Egyptian religion until the reign of Tiberius, whose attitude toward foreign cults was much the same as that of his predecessor. In A.D. 19, the priests of Isis were expelled; the linen vestments and all their other materials were burned. By combining the accounts of Tacitus and Suetonius we get the impression that Isiacs were given the opportunity of recantation, and that they would have to give evidence of it by burning their cult objects.

Quite another story is told by the Jewish historian Flavius Josephus, whose narrative bears all the marks of the romantic style he often affects. His story, highly colored and wrongly inserted among events of about A.D. 30, is open to considerable question. A certain man of equestrian rank, named Decius Mundus, was so smitten by Paulina, the wife of the emperor's friend Saturninus, that he offered her 200,000 denarii (about a hundred thousand dollars) for the privilege of intercourse. Since she was independently wealthy, she refused. A freedwoman named Ida then informed Decius Mundus that she could procure Paulina for only 50,000 denarii, and he accepted her offer. Ida knew that Paulina was an Isiac, and she offered the priests 25,000 as a down payment, with the rest to come later. They fell in with her plan, and the "most reverend" of them informed Paulina that she was to have the privilege of union with the god Anubis. Delighted with the prospect, Paulina went to sleep in the temple of Isis, and without benefit of illumination was united with Decius Mundus. The story got out either through the more naïve priests or through the most naïve Paulina. On the third day afterward, Decius Mundus met Paulina and crudely (and inaccurately) informed her that she had saved him 200,000 denarii. Not unnaturally, she complained to her husband, who in turn complained to the emperor. After investigation Tiberius had the priests crucified, the temple destroyed, and the image of Isis thrown into the Tiber. The moral comes at the end: "He honored Mundus with exile, since he considered as a hindrance to greater punishment the fact that his offences had been offences committed with love."

Several comments may be made on this story. In the first place, it is a fact that in the year 19 Tiberius was concerned with suppressing a tendency toward prostitution on the part of high-born Roman women. The most prominent case also involved a complaisant husband who was exiled. Something of this historical information may be present in the story in a distorted form. In the second place, nothing could be more alien to the policy of Tiberius than the singular moral given at the end. It suggests a view of *le crime passionnel* not common in ancient Rome, and like Luke 7, 47 ("her sins, which are many, are forgiven, for she loved much"), does not really fit the story to which it is appended. Actually it reflects the view of life common enough in the Hellenistic romance. In the third place, the story as a whole is quite similar to the legend of the Egyptian magician Nectanebo and his cautious rape of the mother of Alexander the Great. Thus in some ways the story fits the historical circumstances and in more ways it does not. The degree to which it has been embellished in oral transmission is hard to ascertain. As romantic stories go, it is not unlike the one about Salome's dance in the synoptic gospels. Like Salome's dance, Paulina's seduction may be largely authentic. We cannot be sure of the details.

It remains a fact that a decree of the Senate was directed against Egyptian religion; and in a book dedicated to Tiberius, Valerius Maximus places his account of the action of Aemilius Paulus in a chapter on superstition, while he also speaks with horror and regret of Volusius' flight wearing the head of Anubis.

During the brief reign of Caligula (37-41) came the triumph of the Egyptian religion. Probably after the death and deification of his favorite sister Drusilla, who became *Panthea*, he constructed a new temple of Isis in the Campus Martius, and in an addition he made to the palace of Tiberius there is a room whose decoration is entirely based on Isiac themes.

Under his successors the Egyptian religion was regarded with increasing favor. Otho went too far when he wore linen vestments and celebrated the rites of Isis himself, but when Vespasian went to Alexandria in the year 70 in order to secure Egypt, he received favorable omens in the temple of Serapis. Moreover, the god Serapis (presumably through his priests) encouraged people to come to Vespasian for miraculous cures. Vespasian's first reaction was ridicule and rejection, but the cures actually took place. On their return to Rome both Vespasian and his son Titus spent a night in the temple of Isis.

During the chaotic events of 69, when the temple of Jupiter Capitolinus was burned, the young Domitian escaped from the troops of Vitellius by imitating the action of Volusius. Concealed in Isiac vestments, he mingled with the priests (who were perhaps dismayed by the burning of their own temple on the Capitol) and escaped across the Tiber. During his reign as emperor he rebuilt the temple of Isis.

We hear of no further attempts to suppress the Egyptian religion until the triumph of Christianity. In fact, the coinage of the emperors of the second century and later reveals an almost constantly increasing approval of Serapis and Isis, and in the early third century the Christian apologist Minucius Felix rightly observes that "these rites formerly Egyptian are now Roman as well."

Roman acceptance of Egyptian religion was due almost entirely to popular pressure. The people generally could not find what they had come to want in religion in the old Roman abstractions and state-controlled ritual. They wanted mythology and images; they wanted gods who took a personal interest in them. Such things were provided by the priests of Isis, proud of the antiquity of their religion. To be sure, Serapis had no myth; there was only the official legend of his discovery by Ptolemy I, king of Egypt. But Tacitus, in giving an explanation of Vespasian's visit to Alexandria, was aware that there were those who placed his origin in a more remote antiquity; and Athenodorus, the teacher of Octavian, held that Serapis had been worshiped in Egypt more than three thousand years earlier. As Clement of Alexandria says, Athenodorus wanted to "archaize Serapis," presumably in order to make his worship more acceptable at Rome.

In spite of the rejection of Egyptian religion by the old aristocracy, who were almost unalterably opposed to religious innovation, the cult continued to exist and finally triumphed in the reign of Caligula, to whom many religious novelties are due. After his time there was no question about its acceptance, although the ground for acceptance had been broken with the Senate's action in 43 B.C. On an altar dedicated to Augustus by a freedman in A.D. 1 is an inscription which mentions Isis among the other gods.

In 212, when Caracalla extended citizenship throughout the empire, he admitted the Egyptian gods officially within the *pomerium* and took part in the rites himself. Like Volusius, two centuries and a half earlier, he wore the jackal's head; but times had changed.

4 *Four Roman Theologians and the Divine Julius*

IN THE CIVIL WARS AT THE END OF THE REPUBLIC THERE WERE, AS WE have seen, efforts to suppress foreign religions, even though in the case of the Egyptian religion the prohibitions were repealed after Caesar's death. The Roman senatorial tradition was one of hostility to foreign cults, except when they were directly controlled by the state. On the other hand, the common people seem to have heard foreign priests and prophets gladly. Thus Roman official religion was essentially the religion of the aristocracy. It was exceedingly conservative, and admitted new deities only when political circumstances made such admission imperative. Foreign religions found favor among the masses and among slaves, and naturally lent themselves at least to the appearance of subversiveness.

We have examined the events of the years leading up to the end of the republic. Fortunately, we also possess at least fragments of the work of four members of the Roman aristocracy in which their views on religion are expressed. The earliest is the treatise *On Nature* by T. Lucretius Carus; it was probably published in 54, after Lucretius' death, by Cicero and his brother. Dedicated to an enthusiastic Epicurean, C. Mummius, it presents the traditional Epicurean view of religion and nature in magnificent hexameters which make it one of the classics of Latin literature. Epicureanism had been gaining adherents at Rome, partly among the lower classes but primarily among the aristocracy. In his poem Lucretius identifies religion with superstition and praises Epicurus for freeing men from it. Nature takes the place of the gods.

Slightly later come the works of P. Nigidius Figulus, praetor in 58 and an opponent of Caesar, who banished him. Nigidius was a devotee of magic, Neopythagoreanism, and Oriental religions, all of which he tried to combine with Roman traditions by the use of etymology. His influence was not great since he so plainly supported what the Roman aristocracy rejected.

The most important theological works of the periods were those of M. Terentius Varro and M. Tullius Cicero. The antiquarian and librarian Varro dedicated his treatise *On Human and Divine Antiquities* to Julius Caesar, *pontifex maximus*, about the year 47. He wrote first on human antiquities since, as he said, the divine ones had been instituted by men. In the course of an elaborate analysis (in sixteen books) of gods and their cults, he differentiates three kinds of theology: these are "mythical," "civil," and "natural." This division, he says, was already made by the pontifex Q. Mucius Scaevola, who died a generation earlier. Varro proceeds to develop a system from the division. Mythical theology is suitable for the stage (poets), civil for the state (people), and natural for the universe (philosophers). Only the third type possesses a true insight into the nature of the gods. In the first kind, many things are said which are opposed to the dignity and nature of the immortal gods, especially such things as the legends of their births and the descriptions of their behavior The poets place the gods on a level lower than men. The second is useful for priests and people to know for the performance of civic rites. But the third really explains who the gods are and what their nature is. Ultimately there is one god, the god of philosophers, Jupiter of the Romans, who is also the god whom the Jews worship without the use of images. Here Varro relies on the Graeco-Roman philosopher Posidonius, who held that all primitive peoples rightly worshiped God without the use of cult apparatus.

He sharply distinguishes the religious man from the superstitious one. The superstitious man (as Greek philosophers had said) fears the gods (Lucretius called this the origin of religion); the religious man feels awe toward them as toward parents, for the gods are not his enemies but his friends. As examples of superstition Varro apparently cited the Bacchanalia and the Egyptian religion. He was glad that the Senate's approval was required for the admission of gods to Rome.

Finally we have Cicero's treatise *On the Nature of the Gods*, written after Caesar's death in 44 B.C. In three books he sets forth first the Epicurean criticism of theology and the Academic criticism of Epicureanism (Book I), next the Stoic proofs of the existence of gods, and a discussion of their nature, of general providence, and of special providence (Book II), and finally the Academic criticism of the Stoics (Book III). Cicero is deeply influenced both by the Stoic view and by the Academic criticism of it, and he comes only to a tentative conclusion in favor of Stoicism. He feels that the Roman religion must be upheld in spite of objections, for "without piety, good faith and justice cannot exist and all society is subverted." In writing this treatise he intended to finish his task of presenting Greek philosophy in Latin dress, and to save mankind from superstition while upholding religion. He could not accept Lucretius' identification of the two; he distrusted the syntheses of Nigidius Figulus; and he felt that Varro had not gone deeply enough into the philosophical problems involved. In an appended work, his treatise *On Divination*, he follows a similar method. First the Stoic defense is presented, then the Academic criticism. Astrology is the only kind of prophecy he can firmly reject. In another treatise, *On the Laws*, apparently published after his death, he urges the rejection of foreign religions, especially the Bacchanalia.

In both Varro and Cicero we see the Roman senatorial attitude fully expressed. Both uphold religion while trying to purify it by the use of philosophical theology. Both reject superstition, for superstition is new and foreign religion, irrational and immoral. Atheists take away both religion and superstition, but only superstition should be removed. This attitude toward superstition remained influential among official circles for many centuries after the end of the republic. In spite of the lapses of emperors and others, it remained the Roman official policy. When Constantius condemned Roman religion in favor of Christianity, he called it superstition.

In the year of Cicero's death (43), however, the Roman republic came to an end. The Egyptian religion was officially recognized, as we have seen. And in the following year action was taken by the Senate which radically altered the character of Roman religion. This action was the deification of the dead Julius Caesar.

Divine honors had long been paid to Oriental kings and even to Roman generals in the Orient, and Cicero had planned to erect a private shrine to his favorite daughter after she died. But the official recognition by the Senate of the deity of a dead Roman was quite another matter. For five years he had been worshiped in the East; now the Senate was to consecrate him in the West. Heaven had already given its decision, for Halley's comet had been visible for a week during the celebration of his funeral. He was given the name Divus ("divine"); the month of his birth was called July; a temple and a priesthood were devoted to him; and an annual day of prayer was placed in the official calendar. He was worshiped with the goddess Roma, and his Genius, or familiar spirit, was admitted to the select company of Roman gods. Oaths could be taken by this Genius.

In the deification of Caesar we see the Oriental influences which he despised entering Rome to do him honor. Popular pressure joined with the policy of the triumvirs to provide a new religious basis for national unity. Just as the Senate had found it necessary to take action in the Second Punic War, so now religious novelty was needed again. On the foundation of the posthumous consecration of the emperor was erected a new religious politics. In later times the Senate consecrated good pro-senatorial emperors and condemned those who disregarded its wishes. Consecration remained an instrument of national policy.

II. THE EMPIRE

1 Piety and Insanity

FOR A TIME AFTER THE MURDER OF JULIUS CAESAR IT LOOKED AS IF the republic might be restored. It soon became obvious that such a move backward was impossible. There were three strong men in the state; Caesar's colleagues Marcus Antonius and Aemilius Lepidus, and his nephew Octavian, who was made his heir in his will. For fourteen years after his death Rome was governed by these men, who inevitably came to contend among themselves for supreme power. Marcus Antonius became enamored of Caesar's sometime mistress Cleopatra, queen of Egypt, as we have seen, and tried to create with her a revitalized Oriental monarchy. After his death Octavian became chief of state, with the backing of the Senate. Lepidus received the relatively unimportant post of *pontifex maximus*, while Octavian's policy was formed with the aid of his friend Marcus Agrippa and the millionaire Maecenas. On Octavian's return to Rome in 28 B.C., he began rebuilding the Roman state. His policy required the enforcement of peace after a long period of wars, a great building program which included the restoration of eighty-two temples, and the strengthening of the old Roman religion.

In 27 the Senate voted him the honorific title Augustus, and declared that he was the *princeps*, the chief magistrate of Rome; the same year the Greek city of Mytilene voted him various honors and provided for later additions "so that he may be deified as much as possible." Such was the response of the East to peace in the West. Court poets quite honestly translated Greek into Roman adulation, for a new age of peace and prosperity had dawned. The republic had broken down under the strain of administering a world-empire. Only a hero could govern the Roman state.

At Rome, though he had been instrumental in the deification of Julius Caesar, Augustus always rejected divine titles and honors, and refused to be addressed as "lord," because the term sounded too much like the Oriental madness of Marcus Antonius. But he had to allow unofficial oaths to be taken in his name, and had to permit the worship of Rome and Augustus in the provinces. His own restrained attitude could not override the need for unity on the basis of religion. Elaborate mythological stories grew up about his supernatural birth. Some Greek cities, perhaps spontaneously, required oaths of loyalty to his person and family.

After Lepidus' death in 13 B.C. he assumed the office of *pontifex maximus*, thus officially symbolizing the unity of the Roman state and the Roman religion. Toward the end of his life he was voted the title "father of the country," and in the Bay of Naples shortly before his death he was hailed by sailors who declared that through him they lived, through him they sailed, and through him they enjoyed freedom and fortune. United in sentiment with the populace, after his death the Senate voted his deification. An equestrian took a solemn oath that he had seen Augustus ascending into heaven just as the legendary Romulus had ascended.

Augustus was opposed to foreign superstitions, which he and his advisers regarded as dangerous to the state. They were likely, in his view, to lead to conspiracy and were of course enemies and rivals of the old Roman gods. Therefore, as we have seen, he and Agrippa tried to keep the Egyptian religion away from the Roman people. As Suetonius tells us, he devotedly supported ancient and traditional worships such as the Eleusinian mysteries, but despised the religions of the Egyptians and the Jews. Political considerations compelled him to confirm Caesar's decrees of friendship toward the Jews, but he forbade Roman citizens to participate in the inhuman religion of the Druids, well known for the practice of human sacrifice.

On these questions his course was governed by his desire to keep the Roman blood free from the taint of foreign or slave mixture; he rarely gave Roman citizenship to foreigners and tried to check the freeing of slaves. Similarly, in order to preserve domestic quiet, Agrippa expelled astrologers and magicians from Rome, and in 13 B.C. Augustus himself, as *pontifex maximus*, reiterated the action taken by the Senate two hundred years earlier. All prophetic books, both Greek and Latin, which were in circulation were confiscated, and only the Sibylline Oracles escaped cremation. These, formerly kept in the temple of Jupiter Capitolinus, were placed in Augustus' new temple of Apollo on the Palatine hill.

His successor Tiberius (14-37) continued Augustus' religious policy. He was active in promoting divine honors for Augustus, but he refused them for himself and for his family. When he was asked to accept such honors for his dead mother he refused, though he came to allow worship in Asia for himself and for his mother, provided that worship of the Senate was associated with it. He rejected the idea of a loyalty oath, though such an oath was actually taken. In fact, in A.D. 18 sacrifices were offered to his Genius at Rome. He refused the titles "emperor" and "father of the country," and did not use the title "Augustus" except in correspondence with Oriental kings and potentates. On the other hand, he vigorously enforced the laws forbidding criticism of the emperor, especially after the detection of serious conspiracies.

Probably at the beginning of his reign he moved against Druidism, and absolutely forbade its practice throughout the empire. After a conspiracy in 16, in which astrologers were involved, a decree of the Senate was passed which expelled all Roman astrologers from Rome and Italy, while foreign astrologers were to be put to death. One Roman, inextricably involved in the conspiracy, was put to death in the old Roman manner. He was thrown over a cliff. At the same time, the decree provided an escape clause. Those astrologers who recanted and promised that they would abandon astrology were pardoned.

Three years later came the scandal at the temple of Isis, as well as another involving Jews. Four ingenious Jews persuaded an ingenuous Roman matron to give them funds for the decoration of the temple in Jerusalem. The funds she provided did not, however, reach Jerusalem. On her husband's complaint to the emperor, Tiberius

ordered the expulsion of all the Jews from Rome. This is what Josephus says, but the fact is somewhat less startling. Actually the practice of Jewish customs was forbidden. Four thousand ex-slaves who
refused to abandon their religion were deported to Sardinia for police duty. Other Jews were ordered to leave Italy unless before an
appointed day they had given up their "profane rites." This decree
applied not only to Jews but also to proselytes. Seneca tells us that
one of the tests made concerned abstinence from certain meats. Since
the Jewish community at Rome consisted of considerably more than
four thousand persons, we must assume that many conformed to the
decree and perhaps many more did leave Italy.

The Jewish apologist Philo informs us that the charges made
against Jews who lived in Rome were false, and that very few were
really guilty. Unfortunately, he does not bother to say what these
charges were. In the absence of other information we can only assume that fraud was the chief problem.

We should notice the provision made for recantation, for in the
case of Isiacs, in the same year, it looks as if they too were allowed
to reconsider their religious sympathies. The burning of Isiac vestments and other paraphernalia looks like the proof which the Isiac
would provide.

The business of taking official oaths by the Genius of the emperor
gradually grew more popular, and when Sejanus, the favorite of Tiberius, was administering the empire for him, such oaths began to
be taken by Sejanus' Genius too. After Sejanus' sudden fall in 31,
when his conspiracy was discovered, oaths were allowed only by
the Genius of Tiberius. Since Sejanus had been bitterly anti-Jewish,
his fall also meant the lightening of pressure on the Jews.

We have an interesting document from the period after 31; this
is the collection of *Memorable Facts and Sayings* by the rhetorician
Valerius Maximus. The book begins with examples of religion, that
is to say, Roman religion, and then proceeds to examples of superstition. By "superstition" Valerius Maximus, who dedicates his book
to Tiberius, means just what the emperor meant. Superstition is foreign religion brought to Rome. He starts with the classic case of the
Bacchanalia, and then tells how a certain Roman official wrongly

tried to use foreign rather than native auspices. His other two examples are the deportation of Chaldaeans and Jews in 139 B.C. and the militant ax-wielding of the consul who began to tear down the temples of Isis and Serapis in 50 B.C. All four examples reflect and support the policy of Tiberius. It was Valerius Maximus who lamented the flight of Marcus Volusius wearing the jackal's head of Anubis.

The later years of Tiberius were spent on the island of Capri, and not unnaturally others thought of seizing power. In 33 a conspiracy was suppressed with great vigor, however, and the corpses of those executed for attacking the emperor's authority were refused burial; instead, they were thrown into the Tiber. Such a punishment was generally regarded as cruel and inhuman. Many must have been pleased when next year the mythical phoenix appeared, or was said to appear, in Egypt. Perhaps a new era was about to begin.

After Tiberius' death in 37 his heir Gaius, nicknamed Caligula from the long boots he had worn as an infant accompanying his father on a military campaign, came to the throne. He was greeted with universal acclaim. Provincials, soldiers, and the urban populace hailed him as a long-awaited prince. The Senate was not so sure, since he was only twenty-four years old, but it decreed that the day on which his rule began should be celebrated as the new birthday of Rome. Various provincial cities voted loyalty oaths, perhaps not altogether spontaneously, since the form of the oath was the same in widely separated instances.

His reign began well; on August 19 in 37 he dedicated the temple to Augustus which Tiberius had built, and he asked the Senate, without success, to deify his predecessor. He refused divine honors for himself. Unfortunately, in the summer of the next year his sister Drusilla, of whom he was perhaps excessively fond, suddenly died and was equally suddenly deified. She was the first woman to be placed among the gods by the Roman Senate, but since in Caligula's opinion she was the universal goddess the action is perhaps not too surprising. At the same time Caligula turned to the religion of Isis, in which he took part in woman's clothing. He built a temple to Isis in the Campus Martius. His palace contained a room decorated entirely with

themes from the Egyptian religion. In his enthusiasm and grief—
we must remember that he was only twenty-five—he came to believe
that if his sister was the universal goddess he was the universal god.
His choice of divine raiment gradually became less discriminating,
and a conspiracy was rapidly formed against him. It failed, however.

Caligula soon became aware that his own deity required Oriental
abasement on the part of his courtiers, and he soon insisted that official oaths be taken by his Genius. The next year some enthusiastic
pagans who lived in Palestine on an imperial estate set up a crude
altar to him, perhaps in order to irritate the Jewish majority of the
population. If this was their goal, they succeeded, for the Jews destroyed the altar. The imperial procurator Herennius Capito immediately sent off a report to the divine Caligula at Rome. The Emperor's response was to order a colossal statue of himself as Zeus
Manifest prepared at Sidon and later moved to Jerusalem. Meanwhile
statues of himself were set up in synagogues at Alexandria by enemies of the Jews.

Caligula's next action was to order Petronius, the legate of Syria,
to take two legions—half the forces in Syria—and proceed to set up
his statue in the temple at Jerusalem. By a long series of carefully
contrived delays Petronius managed to wait until the autumn of 40,
when he finally took his legions back to Antioch and decided to refuse to obey the emperor. Doubtless he was hoping for the crisis at
Rome which might be expected to follow Caligula's erection of a
temple of himself there. Actually, the Jewish king Agrippa, who
happened to be, or said he happened to be, in Rome, was the one
who persuaded Caligula to abandon the project. Caligula's letter instructing Petronius to withdraw crossed Petronius' letter stating that
he had done so. The emperor immediately wrote another letter in-
forming the legate that his usefulness to the empire was at an end
and instructing him to commit suicide. This letter was inexplicably
delayed and reached Syria about a month after another letter which
gave the news that Caligula himself had been murdered in January,
41.

From the end of Caligula's reign we possess a record by Philo of an embassy sent by Alexandrian Jews to the emperor. It is a remarkable document, for while Philo clearly recognizes Caligula's madness, he praises the empire as the true form of monarchy and lauds its extension against the barbarians. Augustus, the greatest of monarchs, brought peace and harmony to the world. The emperor possesses divine attributes, which Philo does not criticize in the least. He adds, however, that the emperor governs by laws and respects the laws of peoples subordinate to him. Perhaps this was the only way in which one could hope to gain Caligula's attention.

Naturally the situation changed with Caligula's death and the almost accidental accession of the elderly Claudius (41-54). Like Augustus and Tiberius, Claudius rejected divine honors, though it is significant that in publishing an edict in which the refusal was expressed the prefect of Egypt referred to "the majesty of our God Caesar." Among Claudius' first acts was the publication of this edict, instructing Alexandrians to leave Jews alone and ordering Jews to stop making trouble in the city. Both sides were to behave with gentleness and mutual consideration. Claudius also gave Judaea to King Agrippa in the hope that a native ruler could bring peace. Unfortunately, Agrippa died in 44, no suitable successor could be found, and the new procurator tried to recover the high priest's robe which had been briefly entrusted to the Jews. A prophet immediately arose to try to restore the kingdom to Israel. We shall discuss his attempt when we deal with the Christian problem.

In the year 47 the eight hundredth anniversary of the founding of Rome was celebrated, and Claudius took advantage of the accompanying wave of religious enthusiasm to ask the Senate for legislation on the official forms of prophecy. He explained that they were being neglected because of the strength of foreign superstitions. The Senate complied by instructing the pontiffs to pay more attention to the retention and strengthening of these prophecies.

Within the next two years constant rioting among the Jewish populace at Rome resulted in an edict by the emperor forbidding Jewish religious meetings. By the Jews, and by some Romans, this edict was construed as the expulsion of Jews from Rome as had been the case in Tiberius' day. Suetonius explains the riots as instigated by "Chrestus." Since Chrestus was the usual Greek pronunciation of the name "Christ," we may infer that the riots were concerned with the question of the Jewish Messiah, and that Christians were involved. Certainly the Jewish Christians Aquila and Priscilla were expelled from the city at this time (Acts 18, 2).

Also in 49 a prominent Roman woman, who had hoped to marry Claudius, was expelled from the city because she had consulted Chaldaeans, magicians, and the oracle of Apollo at Claros concerning the emperor's marital affairs. The principal proponent of this action was (not unnaturally) the empress.

In the same year Claudius enlarged the area of the *pomerium*, the old sacred area of the city, presumably to keep foreign cults farther away from the Capitol. It is sometimes said, on the authority of a Byzantine historian, that he recognized the worship of the Phrygian god Attis, but nothing seems less likely in view of the whole direction of his policy. He sought to bring the Eleusinian mysteries to Italy, but after all, Augustus had been initiated in them.

Three years later a much more vigorous attack on astrologers was made. Furius Scribonianus was expelled from Rome for consulting astrologers about the death date of Claudius, and a severe decree of the Senate provided for their exile from Italy. Perhaps at the same time Claudius entirely abolished the religion of the Druids within the empire; it was not only a superstition, but an inhuman superstition. An unfortunate Roman knight from Gaul was pleading a case before the emperor when he dropped a Druid magic egg concealed in his clothing. It had been guaranteed to provide success in lawsuits, but Claudius had him executed without further discussion.

In the spring of 53 there were troubles both foreign and domestic. With the empress Agrippina, who took great interest in court cases, Claudius heard the complaint of certain Alexandrian leaders against the Jewish king Agrippa II. As it happened, Agrippa was a friend of Agrippina. Because the Alexandrian leaders had killed many Jews, and because one of them lost his temper and called the emperor "son of Salome," they were executed. Meanwhile in Palestine another prophet arose, but we shall discuss his case in the next chapter.

At Rome a certain Statilius Taurus, whose lavish gardens the empress wanted, was accused of extortion in the province of Africa as well as of the use of "magic superstitions." He committed suicide without waiting for the verdict. Statilius Taurus has been associated with one of the chief archaeological mysteries of Rome. In 1917 a subterranean basilica was discovered near the Porta Maggiore; it had been built underground apparently during Claudius' reign, but after a few dedicatory sacrifices of a dog and some pigs it was never used. It has magnificent stucco decorations, still admirably preserved, with themes of death and the flight of the soul. What was it? Carcopino argues at length that it was a Pythagorean "church," but the themes are not certainly Pythagorean. It may have been intended for the practice of magic, with which Pythagoreanism was often associated; and it must be remembered that Roman Pythagoreans were suspected of human sacrifice. On the other hand, it may have been simply an elaborate tomb, never used.

A possible explanation could go something like this. Statilius Taurus had built it both for magic and for his own last resting place. When his inclination toward magic was discovered, he was unable to use it for the first purpose. (We should add that it is outside Claudius' *pomerium* line, so that it would not be officially investigated by the police.) And when he committed suicide, according to old Roman tradition his corpse would be refused burial. Of course, the tradition was not regularly observed, but in this case and under this emperor it may well have been. Perhaps he had been arrested not only because Agrippina wanted the gardens but also because, after the Druid cases, magic was regarded as especially dangerous.

Claudius' enthusiasm for old Roman religion brought its due reward. In spite of his refusal of divine honors he was often treated as divine, and at Colchester in distant Britain a temple was erected to him even in his lifetime. It need hardly be said that the barbarous Britons hated it. After his death his successor Nero took steps to obtain his deification, though there were those who suspected Nero's motives, especially after the court philosopher Seneca produced a burlesque called the *Pumpkinification of Claudius*.

Thus Claudius followed the examples of Augustus and Tiberius. He upheld Roman religion, officially rejected attempts to deify him, and vigorously opposed foreign superstitions. Like Augustus and Tiberius, he tried to suppress astrology and Druidism. Like Tiberius, he expelled Jews from Rome. Because of Caligula's favor toward the Egyptian religion, he was unable to move against it. Moreover, it had strong popular support. His policy combined strong Roman archaism with recognition of political facts.

2 Christians As Conspirators

WHAT WAS TO BECOME CHRISTIANITY WAS FIRST BROUGHT TO THE AT-
tention of the Roman government in the year 30, when a report was presumably sent to Rome by Pontius Pilatus, procurator of Judaea, concerning his crucifixion of a Jewish pretender named Jesus of Nazareth. Pilate had at first been uncertain as to the degree of Jesus' guilt, but under pressure from the local high priest he had agreed to execute him. His report was filed in the archives without comment, for at this time the Roman administration was in the hands of Sejanus, a militant anti-Semite, who undoubtedly favored the use of strong measures in rebellious Palestine. Pilate, however, was not closely related to Sejanus, for he continued to rule Judaea for five years after Sejanus' disgrace. On the other hand, in about 32 the Jews sent a petition to Rome that votive shields should be removed from the old palace of Herod in Jerusalem, and Pilate was ordered to re-move them. In the year 36 his harshness brought about his downfall, for after a series of executions in Samaria Pilate was sent back to Rome by the legate of Syria. He was fortunate enough to arrive after Tiberius' death.

In spite of Pilate's problems, the official record was clear: Tacitus tells us that "under Tiberius Judaea was made peaceful." In the Ro-man archives Jesus was recorded only as a rebel, even though Tertul-lian, writing a century and a half later, imagines that Pilate reported the divine nature of Christ, that Tiberius approved his report, and that the Senate rejected it only because of procedural difficulties. It is hard to imagine any possible historical basis for Tertullian's claim.

Moreover, a series of prophets who arose in Judaea and promised the end of Roman rule undoubtedly proved the correctness of Pilate's judgment. Later procurators felt compelled to use troops to suppress the followers of the prophets; Pilate had nipped revolt in the bud. In short, all the documents in the archives which dealt with Jewish prophets and their followers showed conclusively that they were opposed to Roman power and ought to be suppressed as enemies of the state.

Since the attitude of Roman officials towards Christianity was undoubtedly conditioned by their acquaintance with its background, we must consider the series of revolutionary movements which swept through Palestine after the death of Rome's friend and supporter, Herod the Great.

Herod died in 4 B.C. Once the people were freed from what they regarded as his heavy oppression, the weakness of his sons could not cope with them. Archelaus suppressed Passover riots only by killing three thousand Jews. The governor of Syria hastily sent a legion to Jerusalem, but at Pentecost a Jewish mob took possession of the city. In Galilee a certain Judas broke open an armory to equip his followers, while another revolutionary, Simon, burned the royal palace at Jericho but was killed by the king's archers. Another palace was burned at Betharamptha. In Judaea a shepherd-king arose in fulfillment of Old Testament prophecy; he and his four brothers raised a private army which attacked even Roman troops. In Jerusalem the legion was rescued only when the governor of Syria sent two more legions to its aid. The pro-Roman Sadducees and men of means hailed the Roman governor as their savior, while the revolt came to a bloody end. Two thousand active participants were crucified, and many others, combed from the countryside, were sentenced to life imprisonment.

Nine years later, in A.D. 6, the dissatisfied aristocracy of Judaea and Samaria were able to have Archelaus dethroned and replaced by the direct Roman rule of a procurator. Before his arrival, the governor of Syria ordered the customary census taken; taxation was to be in the procurator's hands. According to the gospel of Luke (2, 2) this was the first census to be taken in Judaea. Naturally, the banner of revolt was raised again, this time by Judas of Galilee and a Pharisaic leader named Zadok. According to rabbinic tradition the famous schools of Shammai and Hillel united (for once) in supporting him, and were joined by the majority of the populace. The high priest Joasar, who had been removed by Archelaus, temporarily recovered power and persuaded others to resist Rome.

Their platform was simple. For the Jews there could be no king but God, and therefore no taxes could be paid to the Romans. They could have added that the temple taxes were bad enough without adding another series of Roman taxes to them.

Roman power, however, was restored; Joasar was again removed from office; the census was taken. According to Josephus a revolutionary party was born, and its efforts continued until the climactic war of 66–70.

Under the procurators Palestine was not entirely quiet. The first one retired shortly after Samaritans placed human bones on the porches of the temple at Jerusalem. Another, Valerius Gratus, was appointed by Tiberius and governed Judaea for eleven years. He found the root of the trouble in the high priest's office, for in his first three years he appointed three high priests. The last of these, Caiaphas, was evidently amenable to Roman notions, for he lasted for eighteen years and retired only when Pontius Pilate, procurator from 26 to 36, was recalled. Pilate was sent out just when Aelius Sejanus, the favorite of Tiberius, was reaching the height of his power at Rome. Sejanus was a militant anti-Semite, according to Philo, and Pilate's harshness in Jewish affairs comes entirely between 26 and Sejanus' fall in 31.

Three examples of his harshness are important for tracing the relations of Rome with Judaism and Jewish Christianity.

In the first place, at the beginning of his administration Pilate disregarded the precedent of his predecessors, who refrained from bringing military standards with the emperor's image into Jerusalem, and had such standards brought in by night. He himself was in Caesarea, but great crowds from Jerusalem came to petition him to remove the standards. First he threatened them with violence; then they responded with passive resistance; finally he had the standards moved. This was hardly able administration.

We may note that his contemporary Herod Agrippa described Pilate as "inflexible, merciless, and obstinate" and mentioned his fear of impeachment on the grounds of bribe taking, insults, robberies, outrages, insolence, constant (judicial) murders without trials, and never ending grievous cruelty. A certain suspicion may be attached to this description, in view of the fact that Agrippa was anxious to obtain Judaea for himself, and finally did so. But one can hardly imagine anyone writing the emperor to this effect unless the facts were fairly well established. The historical episodes of Pilate's career do not bear out the picture of him in the later Christian gospels. These portray him as a friend of Jesus. They are trying to shift responsibility for Jesus' death from Rome to Jerusalem.

The second conflict of Pilate came when he expropriated the sacred "corban" money of the temple and applied it to the construction of an aqueduct to Jerusalem. This action illustrates the Roman view that cleanliness is not inferior to godliness. When Pilate then made a tour of inspection in the city, he was surrounded by a mob which presented petitions to him. He had taken the precaution of stationing soldiers among the crowd with clubs concealed under their civilian dress. At a prearranged signal, they drew the clubs and hammered the crowd. Many Jews lost their lives, and Pilate lost whatever vestige of popular support he may have had. Perhaps this was the occasion when the blood of Galileans was "mingled with their sacrifices" (Luke 13, 1).

On the other hand, when a certain Jesus of Nazareth was brought before him as a revolutionary in the spring of the year 30, Pilate tried to release him in order to win the favor of the populace. Under the influence of Caiaphas, however, and others who explained that a claimant to royal power could not be tolerated, he ordered Jesus executed. Caiaphas may have suggested that letters would be sent to Rome if Pilate did not act in support of the high priesthood (compare John 19, 12).

His third conflict with the Jewish people took place just before Sejanus' downfall. He had set up some votive shields in the old palace of Herod. They bore no pictures, but had inscriptions with the names of the emperor and the donors. When news of Sejanus' fall reached Jerusalem, an embassy was sent to Rome, and Tiberius ordered Pilate to remove the shields at once and set them up in the temple of Augustus at Caesarea.

Pilate's ultimate recall was due to his zeal. A Parthian war was being planned in 36, and a legate named Vitellius (later emperor for a few months in 69) was sent out to Syria to direct operations. When a Samaritan prophet gathered a great crowd on Mount Gerizim, Pilate exceeded his authority by having many of them killed and many imprisoned. Perhaps Caiaphas had suggested this move against the Samaritans. In any case, the Samaritans complained to Vitellius, who instructed Pilate to return to Rome. He was fortunate enough to arrive after the death of Tiberius, as we have already observed.

Vitellius himself visited the Passover festival of 37, remitting some Roman taxes and returning to the temple the high priest's robe, which the procurators had safeguarded except during the major Jewish festivals. He was in Jerusalem when the news of Tiberius' death reached him, and the Jewish leaders responded to the opportunity of being the first nationality in Syria to take the loyalty oath to Gaius Caligula and offer sacrifices for him. Unfortunately, as we have seen, the period of calm and friendliness lasted only eighteen months. Then Caligula's conviction of his own deity made peace impossible, though both Vitellius and his successor Petronius remained on excellent terms with the Jews.

Under Claudius, Judaea was governed first by the pro-Roman king Agrippa. Agrippa's friendship to Rome came in question, however, when he began to fortify Jerusalem, and after his death in 44 Judaea was placed under procurators once more. Since Agrippa had been regarded as the restorer of the kingdom of David, even though he was not purely Jewish, the new procurator seemed to violate the prophetic spirit of the Jewish religion. Riots immediately followed his arrival. A prophet named Theudas ("God-given") assembled many followers by the Jordan River. He informed them that at his command the waters would part and they could march through, presumably to Jerusalem. The procurator did not wait to see whether this miracle would take place, but sent a cavalry troop which killed many of them and captured others before Theudas could produce the desired results. Theudas' head was taken to Jerusalem. Presumably he had intended to reproduce the achievement of the Old Testament Joshua.

Again, in about 53 an Egyptian persuaded four thousand men to come to the Mount of Olives outside Jerusalem. At his command the city's walls would fall. The command was anticipated by a Roman attack, in which the Egyptian lost six hundred of his followers and disappeared into the desert, presumably to await further revelation. Several years later the Romans were still looking for him, and the Christian apostle Paul vigorously denied that he was the same person (Acts 21, 38). Once more we have an imitation of Joshua, for it was Joshua who could make a city's walls collapse.

Within a short time both cavalry and infantry were sent against another prophet who promised "salvation" to those who followed him into the desert. There, he said, he would provide miraculous signs (like those of Moses and Joshua) for his disciples. Unfortunately, all of them were killed.

All this material, presumably reported to Rome and filed in the archives, could have been extremely damaging to Christians, even though not all of them took part in such uprisings. The apostle Paul warns the Thessalonian Christians against the notion that Jesus (Joshua) has already returned (2 Thessalonians 2, 2). The "little apocalypse" in Mark 13, 6, informs Christians in Jesus' name, "Many will come in my name, saying 'I am he,' and they will lead many astray." Similarly the gospel of Matthew (24, 25) mentions those who lead the credulous into the desert. Obviously, Christians are being advised to have nothing to do with these movements. But since a warning was necessary, it is likely that some Christians, at least, were taking part in them.

The Christian religion was thus often associated with revolutionary movements in its native Palestine, and this association influenced the attitudes of government administrators.

The first Christian martyr in the reign of Nero was put to death not by the emperor but by the high priest in Jerusalem. In the year

62 Porcius Festus, procurator of Judaea, died; the emperor proceeded to replace him by sending Lucceius Albinus from Alexandria, and also sent word to Jerusalem that the high priest was to be removed and replaced by a certain Ananias, whose father also had been high priest. The family belonged to the party of the Sadducees; that is to say, they took their stand on the old Jewish law and rejected prophecy of the future as well as any doctrine of life after death. They stood for the orderly administration of Jewish affairs in close collaboration with the Roman authorities.

In the interval between Festus' death and the arrival of Albinus, Ananias proceeded to act with the boldness which Josephus says was characteristic of him. He assembled the Sanhedrin, the highest Jewish court, which was competent to deal with all cases involving breaches of the Jewish law, and brought before it certain persons whom he accused of violating the law. The most important of these men was James, the brother of Jesus. The Sanhedrin voted their conviction, and Ananias proceeded to have them stoned to death. We do not know what their offense was. None of the offenses punishable by stoning listed in the Mishnah seems directly relevant; and apparently they did not seem relevant to certain influential Pharisees in Jerusalem. These persons secretly wrote to the emperor asking him to forbid Ananias to act in this way. We may recall that in the Mishnah the milder penalty of "extirpation" (excommunication, so to speak) was provided for most of the offenses also punishable by stoning.

A further problem must have been created by the general principle that only the procurator had the right to inflict the death penalty; but this principle had already been violated in the case of the Christian Stephen. Protests were made when persons unjustly executed had influential friends. In any case, during the absence of a procurator the high priest and Sanhedrin must have believed that they could inflict the death penalty.

On July 19, A.D. 64, a fire broke out in Rome which destroyed a large part of the city. Religious measures were taken to calm the excited populace. Offerings were made to the gods; the Sibylline Books were consulted; prayers were offered to the underworld deities Vul-

can, Ceres, and Proserpina; sacrifices were offered to Juno, first on
the Capitol and then at Ostia. In spite of these ceremonies, there was
a persistent rumor that the emperor Nero himself had been responsible for the fire, since he needed space for the construction of his
new palace, the Golden House. In order to quell the rumor, Nero
accused the Christians of being incendiaries, and put them to death
with unusual punishments.

The Christians, as Tacitus observes, were already the object of
popular hatred because of their crimes. Their founder had been
punished under Tiberius by his procurator Pontius Pilate; the hate-
ful superstition had been temporarily suppressed but broke out again
and not only spread throughout Judaea but, like other subversive
movements, reached Rome. Tacitus elsewhere says that under Tiberius there was peace in Judaea. Evidently he regards Roman Christianity as a relatively recent development.

After his digression on the origin of Christianity, Tacitus proceeds to describe the penalties inflicted on the Christians. The first
group to be arrested confessed—either that they were Christians or
perhaps that they had actually been incendiaries—and gave information about others, a "great multitude," in the case of the Bacchanalia.
All these were convicted of incendiarism and of "hatred of the human race," an accusation often brought against Jews in this period.
Some were dressed in skins of animals and torn by wild dogs; others
were crucified and burned in Nero's gardens while the emperor
drove among the audience dressed as a charioteer. His strange behavior finally excited some sympathy for the Christians, or at least some
suspicion of his motives.

There was nothing remarkable, except for its cruelty, about the
burning of the Christians. An old law set forth in the Twelve Tables
provided for the burning of incendiaries who set fire to a temple or
to a field next to a house, and this law was evidently invoked. More
remarkable was the use of wild animals, perhaps derived from Nero's
enthusiasm for strange mythological games.

It is hard to tell whether any Christians had actually been incendiaries. It is easier to suggest that they may have seen in the fire a sign
of divine judgment upon the city, and that they were probably not

eager to assist in putting it out. Their negative attitude could have been taken as a proof of their hatred of mankind, their inhumanity.

Suetonius tells of the punishment of Christians, but does not connect it with the fire. He says simply that the Christians espoused a "new and harmful superstition." Since, however, his account is more topical than chronological, and since even Tacitus expresses doubts as to the justice of Nero's procedure, we may assume that the persecution was in fact based on the fire at Rome.

This is the first example of Roman persecution of Christians. It was persecution based primarily on the exploitation of popular prejudice. The Christians were scapegoats for Nero. The result was somewhat mixed. A precedent was set for later anti-Christian activities, and their name was darkened in official memory. On the other hand, Nero himself did not escape suspicion, and his cruelty seemed unnecessary at least to Romans who opposed tyranny.

In the confusion of the end of Nero's reign and the civil war which followed, foreign religions played a considerable part. In 65 it was proposed to the Senate that a temple be erected to "the divine Nero," but since Roman tradition provided only for the deification of dead emperors at Rome, Nero refused this doubtful honor. He was content with the erection of a colossal statue of himself, a hundred feet high, in his new palace, the Golden House. (Vespasian removed the head of this statue and replaced it by Sol-Apollo; he set it in the Via Sacra.) Meanwhile the emperor was discussing his future with astrologers, some of whom told him that he would lose his throne but would replace it with a kingdom in the East, perhaps in Jerusalem. Others gave his enemies the same information and were denounced. Confirmation of the Jerusalem possibility was given in the year 66, when the customary sacrifices for the emperor at Jerusalem were suspended and the Jewish war began.

In the year 65 a conspiracy against the emperor was detected; among the more prominent persons implicated was Nero's old tutor Seneca, who at the beginning of his reign had addressed two books *On Clemency* to him. In the second book he had warned against cruelty, describing it as harshness and insanity, and giving as an example the savagery of those who, not content to kill, burned their enemies alive. In his farewell remarks to his friends Seneca spoke of the "savagery of Nero." One may suppose that he had criticized the burning of Christians.

Nero's own religion was simple: he despised all the cults, as Suetonius tells us, except that of the Syrian goddess, but ultimately he came to despise her too. A certain plebeian had presented him with a small image of a girl, as a preventive of conspiracy; and when a conspiracy, perhaps that of the year 65, was detected Nero began to offer sacrifices to the image three times a day in the hope that further prophecies would be forthcoming. In 66 magi brought by Tiridates of Persia admitted Nero to their communion. A few months before his death he attended the rites of the official haruspices, but no favorable omen was forthcoming.

Nero's unenthusiasm for religion may well have been taught him by Seneca, who wrote a treatise *On Superstition* in which he criticized not only mythology but also traditional Roman religion. He attacked the cult of the Great Mother and the "madness" of the other cults on the Capitol, though he admitted that the wise man should observe the rites required by law even though they did not provide pleasure to the gods. He also attacked Judaism and especially its notion of the Sabbath which wasted a seventh part of human life. It could be said of the Jews, however, that they knew the reasons for their rites, while most people, including the Romans, did not know the reasons for their own religious acts.

Nero seems to have preserved the negative part of Seneca's teaching, but in the troubled last years of his life he began a frantic search for religious security. Superstition rushed in to fill the religious vacuum. At the end all prophecies failed. Condemned by the Senate, Nero committed suicide.

A year of chaos followed. After Galba's murder Otho seized power, and in an effort to gain religious support personally took part in the festival of Isis, wearing the linen vestments of initiates. The goddess could not or would not help him, and he killed himself in April, 69. His successor Vitellius entered Rome in triumph, but his horoscope had been most unfortunate; his parents had always tried to keep him out of public office for this reason. Now the astrologers began to recall his destiny, and he replied by an edict expelling them from Rome and Italy by the first of October. The astrologers immediately posted a parody of the edict. "For the good of the state: Vitellius Germanicus should no longer be alive by the same first of October." The result was the immediate arrest of many astrologers and their execution without trial. The urban prefect Flavius Sabinus, brother of the general Vespasian who was in charge of the Jewish war, tried to persuade Vitellius to abdicate in December, since Vespasian had been hailed in the East as emperor, but Sabinus was murdered on the Capitol, and the temple of Jupiter Capitolinus was burned. In the ensuing confusion Vespasian's son Domitian escaped from the Capitol concealed in Isiac vestments and got away across the Tiber. Evidently the popular strength of the Egyptian religion was very great.

Later in the month an army of Vespasian's supporters arrived at Rome, and on December 20 Vitellius was led through the Forum and killed. Early the next year Vespasian went to Alexandria in order to make Egypt secure. There the god Serapis encouraged him by providing popular acclaim after he had entered the god's temple to offer sacrifices. Vespasian was provided with a vision of a friend in Rome, and also, though at first he doubted his own powers, with the ability to perform miraculous cures. Immediately thereafter letters arrived from Rome with the news of Vitellius' execution, and of his own confirmation as emperor by the Senate.

Many prophecies circulated in this brief period. Galba had seemed to confirm the prediction of a ruler from Spain, where he had been governor for eight years. Pro-Roman Jews and Egyptians united in hailing Vespasian as the long-awaited king from the Orient. Only the Druids were disappointed; in the fire on the Capitol they had seen the portent of the transfer of power from Rome to the countries beyond the Alps.

On their return to Rome both Vespasian and his elder son Titus slept overnight in the temple of Isis, to show their gratitude to the goddess and to preserve the support of the people. Once more the astrologers were expelled from Rome, as well as those philosophers who had criticized imperial power. Later in the year Jerusalem was finally taken and sacked.

Under Vespasian and his son Titus, whose brief reign ended in 81, we hear nothing of any suppression of foreign religions. The Egyptian priests were firmly loyal, and the Jewish historian and politician Flavius Josephus was a court favorite. The Christian community in Jerusalem had withdrawn from the city at the beginning of the Jewish war and thus avoided any conflict with Rome.

Toward the end of the reign of Domitian (81-96), however, Jews and Christians were brought into conflict with an emperor who had come to regard himself as divine. The beginning of the conflict may be marked by an edict of the year 89, by which Domitian expelled both astrologers and philosophers from the city of Rome. Presumably both groups were critical of his regime. The climax came in the years after 93, when courtiers and court poets were assiduously flattering the emperor and addressing him as "Master and God." In 93 the edict against astrologers and philosophers was published again, and two years later the consul Flavius Clemens was accused of "godlessness." Domitian had intended the succession to go to Clemens' two young sons, and had appointed the famous rhetorician Quintilian as their tutor. With the emperor's attack on their father, the boys disappear from the pages of history. Clemens was executed and his wife Flavia Domitilla, Domitian's niece, was exiled. At the same time many others were accused of godlessness and of following Jewish customs. Quintilian hastened to express his adulation of the emperor and his contempt for the "pernicious race" of the Jews and their superstition.

After the year 70 the temple tax of the Jews had been paid to the treasury of Jupiter Capitolinus and the emperor; now Domitian moved against those who did not pay the tax but either "lived a Jewish life" or concealed their Jewish origin. Investigations of both circumcision and property holdings were made, and thus an attempt was made to differentiate Jews from proselytes and Christians. We know that some Christians were investigated as Jews.

It is possible that the consul and his wife were Christians, for a Flavia Domitilla later gave a cemetery to the Roman-Christian community. But the investigation was not directed primarily against Christians as such. It was intended to prevent conspiracy and increase revenue. Along the way, Christians necessarily became involved. Perhaps it was at this time that the New Testament books of Luke and Acts were produced. It has been shown that they try to prove that Christianity was a true and pure form of Judaism and that, while often attacked by Jews, it had always been favored by Romans since it was not hostile to the state. On the other hand, Acts clearly depicts the dire fate of a king who imagined himself to be God (Acts 12, 20-23).

Certainly some troubles afflicted the Christian church at this time, for they are mentioned by Clement of Rome at the beginning of his letter to the Corinthians. And "at the end of the reign of Domitian," as Irenaeus says, there was produced a fiery apocalypse which did much to harm the Christian cause. This was the Revelation of John, sent by a seer in exile on the island of Patmos to the seven most prominent churches of Asia Minor. In it he speaks of Jesus Christ as "the ruler of kings on earth," refers to Pergamum, the Asiatic center of the imperial cult, as the place "where Satan's throne is," attacks those at Philadelphia who "say that they are Jews and are not" (a reference to Domitian's decrees), and cryptically refers to a beast which enforces its own worship. This beast has a cipher (666) which clearly refers to the emperor Domitian. He predicts a Parthian victory ("the kings from the East") and the total destruction of the "great city" of Rome, seated on seven hills. Then will come the rule of the "King of Kings and Lord of Lords." When the seer falls down at the feet of an angel to worship him, the angel replies, "You must not do that, (for) I am a fellow servant." Worship is due only to God.

One can only assume that in the province of Asia an enthusiastic proconsul had taken upon himself to enforce Domitian's edict with some vigor. The reason for John's banishment to Patmos remains obscure; perhaps, in view of traces of astrology in his book, discussed by Boll and Lohmeyer, he had been banished from Rome in the year 93. His "revelation" is full of hatred for Rome, and one can imagine that the relatively wealthy churches of Asia, which he tried to arouse, received his book without excessive approval. They may have been impressed with his allusion (Rev. 6, 6) to complaints against Domitian's crop-control legislation of the year 92; "what seemed to be a voice in the midst of the four living creatures" confirmed their belief in unlimited production.

We may perhaps believe that some Christians supposed it necessary to publish an entirely different explanation of the Christian religion, the gospel of John, in which the otherworldly nature of Christianity was stressed and in which it was stated that the authority of the Roman government was given it by God. Jesus did not suffer as a criminal but as a divinely predestined victim of Jewish malice. Had he not been crucified he could not have drawn all men to himself. And in the gospel of John there remain hardly any traces of the primitive Christian eschatology. The gospel has become something beyond and almost unrelated to human affairs.

This book, however, did not appear soon enough to have any influence on the attitude of the Roman government. Accusations on the grounds of "godlessness" and of "the Jewish life" were absolutely forbidden during the brief reign of Nerva (96-98), but the Christian question, once raised, could not be dropped.

By the end of the first century, then, records began to accumulate in the imperial archives which clearly show that there was a tradition of suppressing various kinds of foreign religions. Under Augustus, Tiberius, and Claudius the practices of the Druids had been entirely abolished; under Tiberius, Caligula, Claudius, Nero, and Domitian there had been troubles with the Jews, either in Rome or elsewhere; and under Tiberius, Claudius, Nero, and Domitian there had been difficulties with Christians, though as Jews or incendiaries rather than as Christians. But in order to explain the intermittent prosecutions of Christians in the second century, it seems necessary to suppose that some explicit legislation was provided either by an emperor or by the Senate.

Precedents for such action and for intermittent enforcement were to be found in the case of the Bacchanalia, where the Senate's decree provided that "there should not be Bacchanalia either in Rome or in Italy"; and in the case of the philosophers and rhetoricians in

161, where the decree provided that they "should not be at Rome." Precedents for extermination without the possibility of recantation lay in cases where immorality or sedition was combined with religion, as in the examples of some Bacchants, the Egyptian priests expelled under Tiberius, and the Roman Druids. Precedents for suppression with the possibility of pardon through recantation existed in the cases of the expulsion of astrologers, Jews, and Isiacs under Tiberius, and of Jews under Claudius. As long as Christians seemed to belong to a Jewish sect the manner of their treatment remained in doubt; and this doubt persisted throughout the first century. Under Claudius they were treated as Jews; under Nero some Christians were dealt with separately as incendiaries (perhaps Nero did not at the moment wish to offend his pro-Jewish wife Poppaea); and under Domitian they were treated once more as Jews or proselytes. In Christian literature toward the end of the first century the same confusion exists. The gospel of Luke and the book of Acts try to show that Christianity is the best of the Jewish sects and that it has always been protected by Roman authorities on this basis. The Apocalypse of John is essentially Jewish in form and in content. The letter of Clement of Rome does not go far beyond Hellenistic Judaism.

In the reign of Trajan, however, it finally became possible to distinguish Christianity from Judaism, partly because the Christian church itself became more self-consciously non-Jewish, as in the letters of Ignatius, and partly because greater care was taken in official investigations. With the growth of the imperial bureaucracy there was time to go into these cases more deeply. And as the empire at last became stabilized it was necessary to go into them in order to make sure that movements actually or potentially subversive did not continue to exist.

One must probably assume, therefore, that the crucial legislation intended to assure the destruction of Christianity came from the reign of Trajan, and that it is reflected in the letters of Pliny and Trajan. Two points are clear from this correspondence. Investigations of Christians are relatively novel, for the lawyer Pliny has never attended one. And the basic legal decision had already been made. In his reply to Pliny, Trajan reminds him that "Christians must be pun-

ished." Whether the legislation was in the form of a decree of the
Senate or in that of an imperial rescript cannot be determined, although the later evidence suggests that it was from the Senate. Tertullian rightly summarizes it when he says, "Christianity is illegal."

The precise historical occasion for this legislation is suggested by
the time of its origin. We may suggest that it was due to the discovery of the Apocalypse of John, which had been written at the end
of the reign of Domitian. This document, as we have seen, is mili-
tantly anti-Roman. Though its author affects a dramatic apocalyptic
style with much use of enigmatic expressions, the enigmas must have
been as easy for Roman police officers to decipher as they are for us.
The mysterious cipher 666 plainly refers to Domitian, and the statement that Jesus, who would soon come again, was King of Kings
and Lord of Lords, could mean to a Roman only that he claimed
authority higher than that of the emperor.

The author's gloating enthusiasm for the imminent victory of
Parthia and the collapse of Rome could mean only that he and those
who received his book (the Christians of seven cities in Asia Minor)
were not only potentially but also actually subversive.

The delay between the writing of the Apocalypse and Rome's response could be due to several factors. The Christians who received
it may well have tried to keep it to themselves, and may well also
have tried to explain it away. There was probably some delay while
the document was being examined in various government offices,
and during the last year of Nerva Trajan was propping up the aged
ruler's regime in other ways. Once it had come to the attention of
the emperor and the Senate, however, their reaction must have been
prompt and decisive. Christianity had to be suppressed.

Finally, while it must be admitted that the Apocalypse is ultimately
a subversive document (it may well be a revision of a Jewish subversive document of the time of Nero), it must also be admitted that
its author was right on one basic point. In the long run no compromise was possible between those who recognized no power beyond
the Roman state and those who held that the state, like any other human creation, was subject to a judgment whose ground lay hidden
beyond history. Rome had what were called good emperors, those

who recognized their own limitations and worked in some kind of harmony with the Senate. Rome had so many emperors who were called bad, those who recognized no limits to their own pride and power, that one can only suspect that something was basically wrong in the Roman system. We shall discuss this topic more fully in our closing chapters.

The author of the Apocalypse exaggerates, dreams, hates. What he hates, however, is what all thoughtful Romans hated—the deification of a living man who recognized no limits to his power. At this point we see the tragic element in what he achieved. Roman authorities necessarily concentrated on the form of his message and declared Christianity subversive and illegal. They were blind to the truth of its content.

3 Superstition Suppressed

EVERY STABLE GOVERNMENT COMES TO BE DIRECTED BY A GROUP OF OF-ficials who know one another well and share a common attitude toward the problems facing the state. In the reigns of Trajan and Hadrian, both of whom favored the development of bureaucratic administration, there were many men who held high office and worked well together. For them the divinity of the emperor was es-sentially a useful device for promoting loyalty; they were glad to be living in the new era after Domitian; and they were eager to take part in the political life of Rome under the new and benign emperors.

The most prominent of these men was the historian Cornelius Tacitus, whose family had perhaps come originally from Gaul. His father-in-law Agricola, a senator, had been legate of Aquitania and consul under Vespasian, and legate of Britain from 78 to 84; there-after he was on the shelf at Rome until his death in 93. The year after Domitian's death Tacitus was temporary consul. He published his *Histories* of the years 69–96 in 106, became proconsul of Asia prob-ably in 112–113, and published his *Annals* of the years 14–69 about the year 115. A brilliant writer, he longed for the freedom once provided by senatorial government and opposed the concentration of power in one man's hands. Presumably he found a balance between freedom and responsibility in the government of Trajan. He approved of the extension of empire to the East.

One of his close friends and correspondents was the less brilliant civil servant Pliny the Younger, whose chief claim to fame lies in his letters, which he himself collected for publication. Pliny was temporary consul in 100, when he delivered his *Panegyric* in praise of Trajan. He entered the college of augurs in 103 or 104, and became imperial legate in Bithynia and Pontus about 111. From this province he consulted the emperor assiduously, and both his letters and the emperor's replies have been preserved. He was completely devoted to the emperor and the empire, and in his *Panegyric* praises him for his rejection of foreign cults. In his opinion a new age had dawned with the death of the tyrant Domitian.

A younger friend of Tacitus and Pliny was the non-political writer Suetonius Tranquillus, a rhetorician of equestrian rank whose career Pliny tried to advance without much success. Under Hadrian he briefly held the responsible position of secretary *ab epistulis*. In this office he was in charge of receiving official letters written to the emperor and of preparing the replies to them. His love of scandal led him to make disparaging remarks about the empress Sabina, and with his patron the praetorian prefect he was dismissed about 122. He then turned, presumably making use of materials from the office files, to write his vivid and entertaining *Lives of the Twelve Caesars*, from Julius to Domitian. It would not have been discreet to carry the study further.

Another friend of Pliny was Minicius Fundanus, of equestrian origin but consul in 107. He was also a friend of the famous literary and religious figure Plutarch, who used him as the best available example in his treatise *On Restraining Anger*. While Plutarch's treatise, like all his works, is based on earlier sources, something of Fundanus' "humanity" is visible. In 124 and 125 he was proconsul of Asia. One more official deserves mention, even though he was not associated with the group we have just described. This is the Bithynian Flavius

Arrianus, who under Trajan heard the lectures of the Stoic Epictetus in Epirus. About 130 he was temporary consul, presumably because of Hadrian's favor, and about 133 he became imperial legate of Cappadocia. In 130–131 he sent Hadrian a letter giving a detailed description of the Bithynian coast of the Black Sea; in 136 he dedicated his *Tactics* to the emperor; and perhaps about 137, on his recall from Cappadocia, he published his notes on Epictetus' lectures. Later he retired to Athens.

This is a representative group of the officials who governed the empire in the first third of the second century. Through them the will of the chief of state was made known to the people. Working harmoniously with the emperor, they endeavored to provide peace and prosperity for the vast areas now under Roman rule. In general they shared the emperor's attitude toward strange and foreign religions. Trajan, we know, was opposed to them and favored traditional Roman religion; at his accession his predecessor Nerva was "consecrated" and his ashes placed in the mausoleum of Augustus. Moreover, while Trajan's wife Plotina was hailed in Egypt as "the newer goddess Aphrodite," she herself was an Epicurean. And though Hadrian was initiated at Eleusis, his primary concern was with the restoration of Roman temples and with the building of the great temple of Venus and Roma. He rebuilt the Pantheon of Marcus Agrippa. Finally, both Trajan and Hadrian were engaged in bloody wars to suppress rebellious Jews, and certainly in the second war "superstition" was involved.

We must now consider the attitudes of the officials we have mentioned toward foreign religions. Tacitus clearly regards non-Roman religions as nothing but superstition. He uses this term in discussing the Druids, the Jews, the Egyptians, and magicians. He speaks of the Jewish people as "prone to superstition, opposed to religion." These immoral people "despise the gods" and have an attitude of "hostile hatred toward all other peoples." These remarks are made in his *Histories* of 106. In the later *Annals*, written after he had been in Asia, he speaks of Christians in similar terms. They are characterized by immorality, by hatred of the human race, and by "detestable superstition." So too Pliny, in Bithynia about the same time as Tacitus in

Asia, speaks of the immorality inherent in Christianity, the inflexible stubbornness of Christians, and their "vicious and immoderate superstition." Suetonius too mentions the "new and harmful superstition" of the Christians. Evidently this group of officials had the fixed idea that Christians were both credulous and dangerous, both irrational and immoral.

Their contempt for superstition was common enough in their day. We have an early treatise of Plutarch in which he attacks superstition as almost worse than atheism, and in the contemporary work on gynecology by the celebrated physician Soranus the employment of a superstitious nurse is regarded as likely to bring physical harm to the infant.

What seems singular is their uniform classification of Christianity as superstition. But if we recall the immoderate enthusiasm of many early Christians even after New Testament times, and if we consider their unabated apocalyptic faith, we may see some ground for it. The moderation of a Clement of Rome, writing his disciplinary letter under Domitian, was probably rare. More characteristic was the enthusiasm of an Ignatius, instructing his fellow Christians at Rome not to hinder his progress toward martyrdom.

In any case, as Trajan wrote to Pliny, "the Christians must be punished," even though every opportunity for recantation was to be given them, and anonymous accusations were to be disregarded. This decision required further explanation, and the official who wrote Hadrian about it was Minicius Fundanus. In his time in Ephesus, anonymous documents were no longer presented. His problem was to know whether opponents of Christians could simply hand in signed accusations and leave the rest to him, and whether the tumultuous shouts of crowds in a theater could be taken as accusations. He was evidently anxious to avoid mob pressure, and did not know how to proceed. Hadrian's reply, which we shall presently discuss, showed his successor how to restrain popular demands.

It is a strange fact that in the voluminous works of Minicius' friend Plutarch there is no reference to Christianity at all. He briefly touches on Jewish superstition and is clearly opposed to the imperial cult as practiced under earlier tyrants. Perhaps in the non-theological form in which Christianity was being presented he found it meaningless. Had he known it, he would probably have liked the gospel of John. But he would have regarded the rest of the New Testament as Jewish superstition.

On the other hand, Epictetus, whose lectures received a semi-official blessing, does mention the Christians, whom he calls "Galileans." He is discussing martyrdom before a tyrant, perhaps recalling his own expulsion from Rome under Domitian. He says that reason —that is, Stoic philosophy—can produce inner freedom for the wise man, especially since folly can produce it for an ordinary man, and "habit" for the Galileans. This is hardly a favorable testimony, although the Galileans would doubtless have been flattered not to be regarded as fools. And, after all, another "Galilean" had rejected the opportunity to be martyred with Jesus. But Epictetus is contrasting habit with reason. Not all habitual actions are rational. The actions of the Galileans surely are not.

With this survey of official and semi-official opinion in mind, we can now turn to examine the details of the investigations of Christians made in this period of Trajan and Hadrian.

The relation of Christianity to Rome emerges into clear light in the year 112 or 113, when some Christians in Pontus, on the south shore of the Black Sea, were investigated by the Roman legate. The official before whom they were brought was C. Plinius Caecilius Secundus, who had been sent out as legate of the province of Pontus and Bithynia by the emperor Trajan. As the personal representative of the emperor, he was accustomed to refer delicate problems to Rome, and we possess a collection of more than a hundred letters which he and Trajan exchanged concerning the administration of the province. Among them are his letter concerning the Christians and Trajan's reply. These letters have been called the most important documents of early Christianity outside the New Testament. For our study their significance cannot be exaggerated.

Before examining them we must recall that Pliny was a friend of both Tacitus and Suetonius and that his attitude toward Christianity probably resembled theirs. Both of them regard Christianity as a dangerous superstition, although neither is convinced that Christians were responsible for the fire at Rome under Nero. They know that Christianity is a harmful thing, but they do not accept all the rumors about the behavior of Christians. The same attitude is in fact that which Pliny adopts in his letter to Trajan.

Pliny's procedure is clear and straightforward. Reports have been given him that certain persons are Christians. He summons them and asks them only whether they are Christians or not. If they admit that they are, he repeats the question twice, explaining the penalty for persistence. Non-citizens are executed at once; Roman citizens are sent to Rome. Pliny apparently doubts the truth of rumors of immorality, but argues that stubbornness and inflexible obstinacy certainly deserve punishment.

After the receipt of an anonymous accusation, he summons many more. Some may have been sentenced at once as Christians, though he does not mention them. The others are divided into two groups. The first group consists of those who deny that they are or ever have been Christians. In order to determine the truth of their statement, Pliny gives orders for images of the gods and of the emperor to be brought, and after he dictates the ritual formula they invoke the gods and worship the emperor's image with offerings of incense and wine. They then solemnly curse Christ. These actions prove conclusively that they cannot be Christians (compare 1 Corinthians 12 3). They are therefore released.

The second group at first confesses and then denies. These persons have been Christians—they cannot deny the fact—but they are Christians no longer. They have left the church, some three years earlier, others before then, a few, twenty years past. All these persons prove that they are not Christians by worshiping the images and cursing Christ. Further questioning is needed, however, in order to discover what crime, or perhaps only error, they may have committed in the past. Pliny apparently remembers the principal case which concerns the aberrations of a cult dangerous to the Roman state. He questions them, and reports their answers, in language reminiscent of Livy's account of the suppression of the Bacchanalia.

The Bacchanalia were held secretly and at night. There the priest led the worshipers in a sacred song or incantation; there they swore a solemn oath to perform every kind of crime and immorality. The Bacchants enjoyed wine and feasting and were suspected of cannibalism. In their assemblies men, women, and children took part. The spread of their religion was like that of a contagious disease.

Some picture of this sort was in Pliny's mind as he asked the ex-Christians about the practice of their religion. They replied that they had met before dawn; that they had sung an antiphonal song to Christ (as a god, Pliny adds); that they had indeed taken an oath. The oath was not, however, criminal. It was based on the Decalogue and was a promise not to commit any of the crimes forbidden in the second table of the law. Their meal consisted of ordinary and harmless food, and in fact they had given up the practice of common meals after Pliny's edict forbidding the existence of societies of any sort. (That Christians generally had given up their cult meal may be doubted.)

Because of the evident or apparent harmlessness of these ex-Christians who had proved their loyalty to the empire by obedience to Pliny's edict and conformity to his tests, he decided to check their veracity by torturing two female slaves, confessed Christians of a class which the Christian community called *ministrae* (probably deaconesses; compare Romans 16, 1). Even in their case he found no evidence of immorality. All they confessed was belief of a strange and immoderate kind, which Pliny classified as superstition. Perhaps they spoke, as later martyrs were to speak, of the future resurrection and of the end of the world.

At this point Pliny suspended the proceeding and wrote to the emperor. His letter, and the emperor's reply, deserve full quotation.

It is my custom, master, to refer to you everything concerning which I am in doubt. For who can better direct my hesitation or instruct my ignorance? I have never taken part in private examinations of Christians, and therefore I do not know what crime is usually punished or to what extent they are investigated. I have been very uncertain as to whether allowance should be made for age, and to what extent the weak should be treated differently from the stronger, and whether pardon should result from repentance, or whether it is of no advantage to have stopped being a Christian if a man has ever been one; and whether punishment should be in-

flicted for the mere name apart from crimes, or for the crimes connected
with the name.

Meanwhile this is what I did in the case of those who were reported to
me as Christians. I asked them if they were Christians; if they confessed,
I asked them a second and a third time while threatening them with punishment. If they persevered I ordered them led away [to execution]. I had
no doubt that whatever they admitted, certainly their determination and
inflexible obstinacy ought to be punished. There were others, touched by
the same madness, whom I noted down to be sent to the city because they
were Roman citizens.

Then as usually happens, the progress of the investigation made the accusations more numerous, and more cases arose. An anonymous accusation was brought before me with many names in it. Those who denied that
they either were or had been Christians, I had invoke the gods at my
dictation and worship your statue with incense and wine. I had ordered it
brought into court with the images of the gods for this very reason. Moreover I had them curse Christ; and it is said that those who are really Christians cannot be forced to do any of these things. Others named in the accusation at first said that they were Christians and then denied it, stating
that they had been Christians but had stopped, some three years ago, some
more, and a good many more than twenty years. All these also worshiped
your image and the statues of the gods and cursed Christ. They affirmed
that what their fault or error amounted to was this: on a certain day before sunrise they were accustomed to meet and recite antiphonally a hymn
to Christ (as to a god); they bound themselves by an oath, not for any
crime, but not to commit theft or robbery or adultery, not to break their
word, and not to refuse to repay a deposit. When this was done they were
accustomed to depart and later to meet together for a meal consisting of
ordinary and harmless food. They had stopped doing even this after my
edict in which, following your instructions, I had forbidden societies.
Thereupon I thought it all the more necessary to find out from two female slaves, who were called "deaconesses," what truth there was in this;
and I used torture. But I found nothing but perverse and extravagant
superstition.

I therefore adjourned the examination and hastened to consult you. The
matter seemed to warrant it, especially because of the number of those
endangered. There are many who are and will be in danger, of every age,
from every class, and even of both sexes. The contagion of that superstition has penetrated not only the cities but even the villages and the coun-
try. But it can probably be checked and corrected. At any rate it is clear
enough that the nearly abandoned temples are beginning to be frequented
again, that solemn rites, long interrupted, are carried on again, and that

the flesh of victims is everywhere for sale, although until recently there were few buyers. From these facts it is easy to infer what a multitude can be corrected if there is an opportunity for repentance.

THE EMPEROR'S REPLY

You have taken the proper course, my dear Secundus, in the investigation of the case of those who were accused before you of being Christians. No general rule with anything like a fixed form can be laid down. They are not to be sought out. But if they are accused and convicted, they must be punished, although in such a way that anyone who denies that he is a Christian and proves the fact by worshipping our gods, no matter how much under suspicion he may have been in the past, may obtain a pardon on his repentance.

However, accusations presented anonymously must not be admitted, no matter what the charge is. They follow a very bad example which is not of our age.

In his letter, Pliny says that he has never been present at examinations of Christians. This statement implies that some have taken place, perhaps at Rome, and that he is aware that when Christians are reported to him he ought to hold an examination. He does not know, however, exactly what he is to look for. Therefore he asks the emperor three questions:

1. What precisely is the charge against these people? Is it the mere fact of being a Christian or does it consist of the crimes said to be involved in the fact—crimes for which he can find no evidence? Or is it their stubborn refusal to prove their loyalty by reverencing the image of the emperor? Pliny himself has decided to judge them on this ground.

2. How severe should the punishment be? Should allowance be made for youth or physical weakness? Should recantation be followed by clemency and pardon? Pliny recommends this procedure.

3. Finally, should the Christians be sought out or simply investigated when reported? Pliny's mention of an anonymous accusation suggests that he does not favor searching for them.

The emperor's reply does not entirely clarify the situation. From another letter to Pliny we know that he did not favor accusations based on criticism of the emperor, and he does not mention such accusations at this point. Therefore this is not the charge involved. If the Christian is convicted of being a Christian he must be punished. Trajan assumes that the profession of Christianity is illegal, but does not take the trouble to say why it is illegal. There is no general rule except the basic principle that no one can be a Christian. On the other hand, the state must not take the initiative against Christians. The problems which would result from persecution are more difficult than those caused by the existence of these people. Trajan remembers the excesses of the reign of Domitian.

The severity of the punishment is left to the discretion of the legate, but the emperor agrees with Pliny that recantation automatically brings full pardon. The ground for this decision is already laid in the state's treatment of Jews and astrologers in the first century; Trajan simply authorizes the same procedure in the case of renegade Christians. He agrees with Pliny that a genuine Christian could not worship the Roman gods, while he does not recommend the use of his own image.

Finally, he criticizes Pliny's acceptance of an anonymous accusation. Such accusations recall the atmosphere of the tyranny of Domitian (the "very bad example") and must not flourish in the new age of which Pliny himself had spoken in his *Panegyric*.

The emperor is anxious to provide orderly procedure. His letter does not change the basic fact that those who stubbornly persist in professing Christianity must pay the penalty for their stubbornness.

The other evidence we have from Trajan's reign may help us discover the legal basis of prosecution. According to a Roman Christian half a century later, one of the grandsons of Judas was bishop of Jerusalem early in the second century. Information was laid against him by "the sects" (Jews and perhaps other non-Christians), and he was brought before the ex-consul Atticus, who tortured him for a considerable time and finally had him crucified. If this story is even approximately correct, it shows that the profession of Christianity was illegal.

It is hard to assess the story, because it is hard to tell who the ex-consul was. He was probably Sextus Attius Suburanus, consul early in 101 and again in 104. The date of the martyrdom is difficult to determine, for in his *History* Eusebius apparently dates it in 101, while in his *Chronicle* he puts it in 107, with Ignatius.

If—and this is only a possibility—it took place in 101, it may have some relation to the proclamation of a new remission of sins by the Jewish-Christian prophet Elchasai in the same year. The occasion of this proclamation might be the falling away of many Christians in a time of persecution.

Also during the reign of Trajan, and perhaps at the same time, a bishop of Antioch named Ignatius was sent to Rome. Ignatius' letter to the Roman church is dated, but unfortunately it gives only "August 24" and not the year. He was on his way in the custody of ten soldiers, and expected to be delivered to wild beasts. He asked the Roman Christians not to intercede for him, for he had made up his mind to be ground by the beasts' teeth as the "wheat of God" so that he could become "the pure bread of Christ." He had heard that sometimes they refused to touch their prey, and he stated that he would force them to consume him.

Modern critics have sometimes criticized his "death wish," but since he says he has already been condemned it is difficult to see what the Roman community could do for him. Perhaps they could get him beheaded rather than eaten; his name is the Greek form of a Roman name (Egnatius).

We do not know whether he was sent to Rome as a leader of an outlaw band or as a physical specimen worth exhibiting to the Roman urban populace. In any case, from the contemporary letter of Polycarp to the Philippians we know that other martyrs (whom Ignatius does not mention) were sent to Rome from Asia with him.

The martyrs of Trajan's reign thus include the bishops of Jerusalem and Antioch, but there is no record of the deaths of bishops elsewhere, or indeed of many martyrs anywhere. The emperor's effort to suppress Christianity seemed to have achieved its purpose, although we know that Christians continued to meet, perhaps in secret.

In 115 and 116 his attention was diverted by a series of Jewish revolts. At Cyrene the Jews took vengeance on their oppressors in what seemed cruel and unusual ways. They ate the dead bodies of Romans, and forced living ones into gladiatorial combats or into contests with wild beasts. Obviously they were doing no more than confirming the worst suspicions of Romans or paying back the penalties inflicted on Christians. Perhaps they were Jewish Christians themselves. Trajan himself was in Antioch in 115 (perhaps Ignatius was arrested then), and intended to go to Mesopotamia, where he wanted to establish Roman rule. The Jewish revolt, however, spread through Egypt and Cyprus to Mesopotamia, and overcome by illness Trajan returned to Rome. Armenia and Mesopotamia were lost to the empire.

In Trajan's reign we see the effort of a great administrator to consolidate the gains of his predecessors and to ensure the safety of the Eastern frontier. In his religious policy every effort was made to provide for the unification of the empire. Because of the strength and, indeed, fanaticism of the adherents of Christianity and Judaism his policy, while outwardly successful, did not ultimately work. In the case of Christianity both the emperor and his subordinates were governed by their preconceived notions concerning its nature. They could not recognize that the Christianity of the early second century was in transition and that it had elements within it which could contribute to the unity of the state.

The best example of Christian loyalism is provided by the so-called first epistle of Peter, directed from Rome to the Christians of Pontus, Galatia, Cappadocia, Asia, and Bithynia. The author calls on these Christians for absolute loyalty and obedience to the Roman emperor and his subordinates, thus reiterating the statement of Paul to the Roman church half a century earlier. He urges the preservation of a hierarchical social structure and commands his readers to suffer as Christians, not as malefactors. The address of the letter and the mention of suffering "as a Christian" proves conclusively that it was written (though doubtless with the use of earlier materials) in the reign of Trajan. It came to Asia too late, however, to undo the harm done by the Revelation of John.

Trajan's successor Hadrian (117–138) was interested in all kinds of foreign superstitions, though he was initiated only in the Eleusinian mysteries, following the example of Augustus. His reign was spent on the road, for he was determined to provide good govern-

ment for all the areas of the vast empire Trajan had left him. During
123 or 124 he received a letter from Licinius Granianus, proconsul of
Asia, concerning informers who were accusing Christians. The emperor did not reply, since he intended to visit Asia in the near future.
In 124 Minicius Fundanus, the friend of Pliny and Plutarch, became
proconsul of Asia, and Hadrian addressed a rescript to him.

In this rescript he speaks of the letter of Licinius and states that
he is answering it in order to prevent the activities of informers, who
are essentially nothing but robbers. He outlines the procedure which
Minicius is to follow. Provincials are permitted to bring charges
against Christians and present proofs before the tribunal of the proconsul. However, simple accusations or mob demonstrations are not
allowed. Any accusation must be thoroughly investigated by the
proconsul. If an accuser proves that those he accuses are doing anything contrary to the laws, the proconsul is to set appropriate penalties. On the other hand, if an informer brings charges simply for his
own benefit, he is to be punished all the more severely.

Contrary to what laws? Hadrian's sentence seems to reflect exactly
the same situation as the one we find in Trajan's letter. No fixed form
can be provided, and Christians can be investigated either as Christians or as malefactors. The basic problem for Hadrian is administrative, not legal. We may suppose that there is a law which forbids
the existence of Christians because of their crimes. The proconsul
can take cognizance either of the Christianity or of the crimes. What
he must avoid is the activity of informers.

Since Hadrian was in Asia Minor in the interval between Licinius'
letter to him and his reply to Minicius Fundanus, we may assume that
he had investigated conditions for himself and had discovered that
the danger from informers was greater than that from Christians.
Like Trajan, he could hardly forget the excesses of the reign of
Domitian. He knew that the atmosphere of suspicion and hatred
brought about by encouraging informers was far worse than any
subversive activities the informers might denounce. Hadrian may
have written other letters like the one to Fundanus, as Melito later
says, but Melito may be generalizing from this single case.

In the winter of 124–125 Hadrian was at Athens, where he was initiated into the Eleusinian mysteries. According to Eusebius the apology of the Christian Quadratus was presented to him at this time. Unfortunately only a fragment of his work remains. In it he apparently contrasts Christ with other saviors and argues that only he was divine. Since "savior" was a common predicate of Hadrian, Quadratus' treatise may not have aroused a favorable response.

There is no evidence for any vigorous persecution of Christians in Hadrian's reign. On the other hand, they must have been under some attack since Epictetus speaks of their habitual resistance to one whom they regarded as a tyrant.

In 132 Hadrian decided to rebuild the devastated city of Jerusalem as a Roman colony, calling it Aelia Capitolina. The response of the Jews to this idea was immediate; a rebel arose, proclaiming himself "Son of the Star" (based on a prophecy in the book of Numbers) and gaining great popular support. Even the rabbinic leader Akiba believed that the Son of the Star was the long-promised king of Israel. To suppress the rebellion Hadrian summoned one of his best generals from Britain, and after a three-years' war the Jews were finally vanquished. The Christians refused to join the Son of the Star, and he vigorously attacked those Christians who still lived in Palestine. A papyrus letter has recently been found in which he warns one of his lieutenants against dealings with those whom he calls "Galileans." In the course of the war Jewish Christianity came to an end. At its close Hadrian forbade the practice of circumcision, ordering his subordinates to treat it as a form of castration. This wartime edict, a direct violation of all precedents and treaties, remained in force only for the three years until his death in 138, and was repealed by Antoninus Pius.

A peculiarity of Hadrian's reign was the death and deification of his favorite Antinous. This handsome youth fell into the Nile from Hadrian's barge in the year 130, and the grief-stricken emperor founded the town of Antinoopolis on the shore at this spot, erected columns everywhere with Antinous' portrait on them, built temples and assigned divine honors to him. Greek (not Roman) coins bear Antinous' image and the title "god." Such easy deification scandalized both Jews and Christians.

At the very end of his reign there was a Christian martyr, Telesphorus, bishop of Rome. His death is traditionally assigned to the following year, but since the historian Dio explicitly tells us that Antoninus Pius refused to punish any of those accused at the beginning of his reign, we must assume that Telesphorus was executed the year before. We do not know how he came before the courts, but in any event he was put to death.

Telesphorus is the only martyr whom we know in Hadrian's reign, although Hadrian showed no special favor toward Christians. Presumably he was too busy with other matters, especially with his journeys of inspection all over the empire, to bother with enforcing the laws concerning them. Their loyalty during the Jewish war must have seemed a favorable sign.

4 The Loyalty Oath

THE LONG REIGN OF THE EMPEROR ANTONINUS PIUS WAS NOTED FOR ITS uneventfulness. He was devoted to the state religion. An inscription gives thanks to him as "the best and greatest ruler, most just and most benevolent on account of his outstanding care and religious devotion toward the public rites." His attitude toward foreign religions was one of relative toleration. He removed Hadrian's ban on circumcision, and fairly early in his reign wrote letters to various cities of Asia Minor instructing their citizens not to make innovations or to use violent measures in regard to the Christians. His letters are lost, and we know neither the occasion nor the precise content of his instructions. Probably he simply reiterated Hadrian's policy.

On the other hand, there was a distinguished group of officials under Antoninus whose members clearly regarded Christianity as a dangerous superstition. This group included Cornelius Fronto, famous rhetorician, tutor of the young Marcus Aurelius, consul in 143; Munatius Felix, prefect of Egypt between 148 and 154; and Lollius Urbicus, consul under Hadrian and sometime governor of Britain.

At some point the attitude of these officials became more severely anti-Christian, and we must ask when and why this change took place. The occasion for it probably lies in the circumstances of the Roman church after Telesphorus' sudden martyrdom. Under his successor Hyginus, gnostic teachers from all over the world flocked to Rome. Around this time a minor official of the city erected an altar on the Tiber island to the old Roman deity Semo Sancus Deus Fidius, as a manifestation of sympathy with Antoninus' religious policy. The Simonian gnostics immediately seized upon the inscription as evidence of official approval of their hero. SEMONI meant "to Simon," SANCO meant SANCTO, "holy," and DEO of course meant "god."

Other gnostics arrived with other proposals for the policy of the Roman church. Valentinus urged a world-denying philosophical theology, and Marcion offered a theology which would completely separate the church from Judaism. He was aware of the Jewish troubles related to the Son of the Star, and he argued that there were two gods, one the god of the Jews, whose Messiah obviously had not yet come (though when he came he would resemble the Son of the Star), the other the Father-God, whose emissary had been Jesus. A carefully expurgated Bible could prove this theory and support a religion harmless to the Roman state.

Still other gnostics brought pagan rites which (perhaps like those of the Simonians) strongly resembled the ancient Bacchanalia. Rejecting the Old Testament and the world of matter, they tried to prove their superiority to the world by escape into debauchery.

Since Hyginus was obviously unable to expel these gnostics, it is not surprising that the Roman government was unable to differentiate them from other Christians. Probably at the time of his consulship in 143, Cornelius Fronto produced an oration against the Christians in which he collected all the scandal he knew. His complaint is worth quoting as evidence of what a presumably intelligent Roman could believe:

They recognize one another by secret marks and signs and they enjoy mutual love almost before they meet. Here and there among them is spread a certain cult of lust, and they promiscuously call one another brother and sister, so that their frequent fornication becomes, by the use of a sacred name, incest. Thus their vain and insane superstition glories in its crimes. Unless there were a foundation of truth, wise rumor would not speak of these wicked matters, rightly suppressed. I hear that they worship the head of a most disgusting animal, consecrated by some stupid conviction or other: their religion was born worthy of such customs! Others say they worship the genitals of their leader and priest, and so to speak adore their own source. This may be erroneous, but certainly the suspicion would arise in their secret nocturnal rites. And anyone who tells of a man paying the supreme penalty for his crime, and the deadly wood of a cross in their ceremonies, attributes suitable altars to these depraved criminals. They worship what they deserve. Now the story of their initiating novices is as detestable as it is notorious. An infant, concealed in meal so as to deceive the unwary, is placed before the one who is in charge of the rites. This infant, hidden under the meal, is struck by the novice, who thinks he is striking harmless blows but kills him with blind and hidden wounds. Horrible to relate, they drink his blood, eagerly distribute the members of his body, and are united by this sacrifice and pledged to common silence by this awareness of guilt. These sacred rites are more disgusting than any sacrilege. Everyone knows about their banquet, and everyone speaks of it. People of both sexes and every age come to the banquet on the accustomed day with all the children, sisters, mothers. There after much feasting when the banquet has grown warm and the heat of drunkenness burns into incestuous desire, a dog tied to the lampstand is aroused to run and jump by throwing a bit of food beyond the length of the rope by which he is tied. Thus with the light (a witness to their guilt) overturned and put out, the haphazard embraces of shameful desire take place in the shameless darkness. Even though all may not be incestuous in deed, all are incestuous in conscience, since it is with the approval of all that they permit whatever can happen in the action of each.

It is of course quite possible, as Justin and others suggest, that such activities were actually carried on in gnostic "nihilistic" groups, though Fronto's description seems to owe much to parody and to literary accounts of the Bacchanalia. As a portrayal of the regular meeting of Christian communities it is fantastic.

By the time Munatius Felix was prefect of Egypt, criticism of gnostic conduct was so prevalent that at Alexandria a young Christian asked official permission to be castrated, "in order to prove that promiscuity was not a Christian sacred rite." His application involved little risk, in view of the absolute legal prohibition of castration, but it must have made an unfavorable impression on Munatius

Felix, no matter how splendid the Alexandrian Christians may have considered it.

By about 150 anti-Christian feeling had reached such a pitch that a Christian teacher at Rome believed it necessary to address an official petition to the emperor. His treatise, which displays a marked inability to stick to the point, is actually an official request for two things. One is an official investigation into Christianity which could settle the problem of Christian disloyalty and immorality. Justin tries to describe Christian doctrine as background material for such an investigation. The other is an equally official investigation of the behavior and teaching of followers of Simon Magus, Saturninus of Antioch, and Marcion. Justin disavows them as Christians and states that he cannot vouch for their behavior. As an appendix to his petition he cites the rescript of Hadrian to Minicius Fundanus, in the hope that it will be taken as a precedent for such an investigation.

It seems obvious that such a petition must have been provoked by some fairly official action or pronouncement, and the best possibility for such a pronouncement is the oration of Fronto which we have already quoted. It was published with the authority of an ex-consul who was also the future emperor's tutor. Justin hopes that by addressing Antoninus Pius, the "philosopher" Marcus Aurelius, and the "philosopher" Lucius Verus, he will achieve some results. We know of no official action, but since Christians were not persecuted an investigation was probably made. The emperor was content to let anti-Christian legislation remain valid, although he probably decided to enforce it leniently.

On the other hand, some of Justin's language in regard to the Roman empire is hardly politic, and one can imagine that the emperor's response, when his attention was drawn to such passages by Fronto or others, would hardly be favorable.

Justin's admiration for philosophy is considerably greater than for the Roman government. The emperor is called Pius and his son is called a philosopher; but, says Justin, it is the task of true piety and true philosophy to investigate questions and to act in accordance with truth rather than hearsay. A favorite quotation of Marcus Aurelius was taken from Plato: "Unless the rulers are philosophers, the cities are not fortunate." Justin cites the same words, asking the emperor to prove that he is a philosopher. He states bluntly that the royal family does not investigate the facts, and compares Christians to the martyred Socrates. The royal family cannot even see that Christians obviously do not expect a human kingdom. If this were their goal they would deny when questioned. Since they do not deny and prefer to die, they cannot be revolutionaries.

Actually they are the empire's chief allies in the cause of peace. Their teaching of divine judgment and eternal punishmnt for the wicked is more effective than the enforcement of human laws. "You seem to fear that everyone will act rightly and you will no longer have anyone to punish." Justin evidently assumes that imperial and divine legislation are at least parallel, though the two administrations are quite different.

At the end of a sketch of Christian morality, Justin recalls the teaching of Christ on rendering to Caesar and interprets it, in the light of Romans 13,6, as meaning payment of taxes and service to the state. Christians recognize the authority of the emperors and pray for them, "that along with royal power they may have sober reason." On the other hand, if they continue to despise Christianity, they will receive a penalty in proportion to their power—in eternal fire. All kings die; all men can feel such punishments after death.

The positive rôle of the Roman empire in history is developed only slightly. Bar Cochba, the leader of the Jewish revolt in 132–135, was, like the Romans, a persecutor of Christians. But there could not be a native ruler or king among the Jews because of the prophecy of "Moses" (Genesis 49, 10 LXX) that there would be a Jewish ruler until the coming of "the expectation of the nations." This expectation was Jesus Christ. After he was manifested the Romans took over the government of the Jews, at the time when Titus captured Jerusalem and destroyed the temple.

At the end of his apology Justin repeats the warning he has given earlier. "We tell you in advance that you will not escape the future judgment of God if you remain in injustice." He then adds a copy of Hadrian's rescript in favor of Christians as an example of what just treatment would be.

In Justin's view the only justification there could be for the existence of the Roman empire would be its justice, its punishment of malefactors, and its vindication of Christians. He repeatedly speaks of Jesus as having suffered under Pontius Pilate, and he is well aware that Pilate was the procurator of Tiberius Caesar. He does not seem to expect that justice will actually be done, and his fears were obviously justified since he himself was later put to death by the philosopher-prefect of the philosopher-emperor.

It has often been said that Polycarp, bishop of Smyrna, was put to death during the reign of Antoninus Pius, but we shall see that the true date of his martyrdom is probably February 23, 166, and therefore he was executed not under Antoninus Pius but under Marcus Aurelius.

At some point toward the end of Pius' reign, however, a Christian teacher at Rome was in prison. This was not Justin but a certain Ptolemaeus—possibly, but by no means certainly, the famous gnostic teacher of that name. A wealthy woman to whom Ptolemaeus had given Christian instruction came to practice a new morality, and her morality led her to divorce her husband. In his distress he accused her of being a Christian. She replied with a petition to the emperor asking for a stay while she settled her affairs; this was granted. Her husband then turned his attention to Ptolemaeus, and managed to have his Christianity investigated. The result was that Ptolemaeus and two others were executed by Lollius Urbicus, urban prefect between 144 and 160, probably toward the end of his administration.

Around the same time a Cynic philosopher named Crescens, who had "made a nest for himself" at Rome, was trying to bring Justin and his pupil Tatian before the prefect, but apparently without success.

The long reign of Antoninus Pius meant peace and security for most of the inhabitants of the Roman empire. "All the provinces flourished under him," says the *Historia Augusta*; "informers were extinguished." He was deservedly compared with the legendary king Numa, and two years before his death he restored the temple of Augustus at Lyons. Christians, however, were subject to sporadic investigation, and remained suspect in the eyes of influential persons such as Cornelius Fronto, Munatius Felix, and Lollius Urbicus. The new emperor was to be surrounded by officials who shared his view that they were dangerous.

In the year 161 the new emperor assumed office at Rome. This was the man who is described by a later biographer as one who was a philosopher throughout his life and surpassed all other emperors by his virtue. Marcus Aurelius Antoninus had been brought up under the eye of the emperor Hadrian, who had instructed his adopted successor Antoninus Pius to adopt Marcus in turn. On his deathbed Antoninus confirmed Hadrian's choice (March 7, 161). The Senate agreed and set its seal of approval on the acts of the dead emperor by voting his deification. Marcus took Lucius Verus, who had also been adopted by Antoninus Pius, as co-emperor, and on August 31 a favorable omen took place when twins (one of whom was the future emperor Commodus) were born to Marcus' wife Faustina, the daughter of Antoninus. Coins of the year are inscribed with security, felicity, felicity of the times, and felicity of the age.

It was at this point, apparently, that Justin addressed his second petition to the new emperor. He described the case of Ptolemaeus, which had taken place only recently, and once more insisted on the moral and philosophical nature of Christianity, asking for an investigation and for the publication of the results. In this petition he made considerable use of Stoic terminology, presumably in order to influence the emperor as well as his teacher Junius Rusticus, consul in 162. As far as we can tell, no official reply was made. The question was being investigated, and the answer did not come until the year 166. Justin ascribed the accusations of immorality to tortured slaves, children, or women; presumably further information was needed by the police.

The wars which were to mark the whole length of Marcus' reign soon occupied the attention of the emperors. Lucius Verus turned to the East to make Antioch his base for the campaigns against the Parthian empire, while Marcus devoted himself to philosophy and to administration at Rome. In the East Lucius chose as his commander a determined disciplinarian named Avidius Cassius, who succeeded in

pressing into Armenia (setting a former king on the throne in place
of the Parthian satrap, who was exiled to distant Britain), and finally
reaching even Babylon and Media. The Parthians began negotiations
for peace.

At the end of the year 165, when Roman troops had captured
Seleucia in Assyria, and the image of Apollo Comeus had been
brought to the temple of Apollo on the Palatine, a pestilence broke
out—some said it had come from the temple in Seleucia—and could
not be checked. By the next year it had reached Rome and vigorous
efforts were made to stop its course by religious rites, especially in
view of its possible religious origin. The emperor ordered a lustra-
tion of the city of Rome, along with the *lectisternia* which lasted for
seven days, while he delayed his departure against the Marcomanni on
the Danube. He did not leave the city until the next year.

This *lectisternium* consisted of the arrangement of a couch for a
god or for various gods, in preparation for a banquet dedicated to
him or them. Our sources do not state whether the *lectisternia* of 167
were devoted to the Twelve Gods of Rome or to a single god such
as Apollo, although *lectisternia* for the god of health would certainly
have been appropriate at this time. In any case these were religious
rites proposed by the emperor and as such required the cooperation
of every Roman.

The situation was critical. The plague had proved exceedingly dev-
astating; the "prophet" Alexander of Abonuteichos had provided
talismans, ineffective to be sure, against it; and apocalyptic expecta-
tions were abroad. There is a singular story in the *Historia Augusta*
about a man who climbed a fig tree in the Campus Martius to announce that fire would fall from the sky and the end of the world
would come, if when he dropped from the tree he turned into a
stork. Unfortunately, he fell and merely let a stork emerge from his
clothing. He was thereupon taken before the emperor, although upon confession he was released as harmless.

Not so harmless were the Christians. They had long been predicting the destruction of the world by fire and had doubtless ventured
to see in the plague one of the signs which were to precede the end
of the world (compare Luke 21, 8–11). Perhaps they saw in the fall

of Babylon the partial fulfillment of the prophecies in the Apocalypse of John (17–18). Apparently the coming of the plague and the unsettlement resulting from it were responsible for the troubles of the church in this period. In devastated Asia Minor, Sagaris of Laodicea was martyred when Sergius Paullus was proconsul (some time between 164 and 167). Martyrdoms at Thyatira may have occurred at this time. (Note that both Laodicea and Thyatira are addressed in the Apocalypse.)

Probably in 166 the apologist Justin and six of his pupils were brought before the urban prefect, Junius Rusticus. Like Sergius Paullus, Rusticus belonged to the group around the emperor which shared his interest in philosophy. Like him, Rusticus was consul on two occasions, and Sergius Paullus succeeded him as prefect. When the Christians came before Rusticus they were almost in the presence of the emperor. Rusticus had strongly influenced the young Marcus as his teacher, and had turned him from rhetoric to Stoic philosophy twenty years earlier. Now in old age Rusticus was one of the most highly trusted counselors of the emperor, always greeted in the praetorium before the prefects. Even though Marcus was often annoyed by him, he never let his annoyance carry him too far; Rusticus had taught him to be ready to forgive. After Rusticus' death (168?) the emperor asked the Senate to erect statues to his memory.

Such was the man before whom Justin and his companions were brought, upon their refusal to sacrifice to the gods. Since Justin had taught in Rome for some time without being molested—though apparently he had left the city for a time—we may assume that there was some special occasion for his arrest. He had been active in debating with the Cynic Crescens, and according to Tatian Crescens used the occasion of the plague to effect his purpose.

After a rapid cross-examination in which Rusticus conveyed his contempt for the education and the eschatological hopes of Justin, he came to what he called "the matter at hand, which is indispensable and urgent." The matter was simply the demand to come together with one accord and offer sacrifice to the gods. This requirement had been in effect since the reign of Trajan, when as we have seen his legate in Bithynia and Pontus instituted it as a test of loyalty. Justin

and his pupils rejected it as irreligious and were condemned to death "in accordance with the laws." The fact that they were scourged and beheaded shows that they were Roman citizens of the upper classes.

Probably in the same year, as we have already said, Polycarp of Smyrna was brought before the proconsul of Asia. The authentic kernel of the *Martyrdom of Polycarp* does not give the proconsul's name, and we must derive it from other information. The circumstances of his arrest were as follows. When one of the Christians was in the arena at Smyrna with a wild beast, which refused to eat him, he pulled it toward him in order to finish the affair. The crowd cried out with one accord, "Away with the godless; let Polycarp be searched for." While some Christians took the oath and offered sacrifice, it was well known that Polycarp was "the teacher of Asia, the father of the Christians, the destroyer of our gods, who teaches many neither to sacrifice nor to worship."

The police picked up Polycarp at a farm outside the city, and on their way to the city they tried to persuade him to say "Caesar is Lord" and to offer sacrifice, but he informed them that he would not follow their advice. At the arena the proconsul urged him to take an oath by the Genius of Ceasar and say, "Away with the godless." The proconsul continued his efforts. "Take the oath and I will let you go; curse Christ." Polycarp then professed his loyalty to Christ rather than to the Roman emperor. The proconsul still persisted, and asked for an oath. At this point Polycarp stated plainly what the proconsul had been trying to keep him from stating. "If you vainly suppose that I shall take an oath by the Genius of Caesar, as you say, and pretend that you do not know who I am, listen plainly: I am a Christian. And if you wish to learn the doctrine of Christianity, set a day and listen." The proconsul suggested that Polycarp persuade the people. "You I should have held worthy of discussion," the bishop replied, "for we have been taught to render due honor to princes and authorities appointed by God" (Romans 13, 1; 1 Peter 2, 13). "But as for those people, I do not consider them worthy of an apology." Under these circumstances the proconsul could only ask for recantation and threaten Polycarp with the wild beasts and the stake. Polycarp remained firm, and since the Asiarch refused to supply a lion the bishop was burned alive.

One of the more singular features of this singular story is the expression, "Away with the godless." This does not occur in other accounts of the investigation of Christians, and it seems to reflect the circumstances of Asia during and after the proconsulate of P. Mummius Sisenna Rutilianus (162–163). Mummius Rutilianus was afflicted with religious mania. His critic Lucian called him "the old fool." He came under the influence of Alexander of Abonuteichos to such an extent that at the age of sixty he married the prophet's daughter and took her back to Rome with him. There he introduced Alexander in official circles, and even the emperor followed his counsel by throwing two lions into the Danube to assure victory in 166. Alexander's influence was at its peak, in spite of the opposition of Epicureans and Christians. His "mysteries" began with this proclamation: "If any godless man, either Christian or Epicurean, has come to spy upon the mysteries, let him flee; let those who believe the god [Alexander's pet snake] be initiated propitiously." We know that Alexander remained strong in Asia; the governor of Bithynia and Pontus in 165–166 told Lucian that even if Alexander were caught in the act of murder he could not be punished, because of the influence of his son-in-law.

Polycarp's martyrdom, then, may well have been brought about by anti-Christian enthusiasm instigated by the followers of Alexander. The proconsul (probably Sergius Paullus) was unable to deny the mob its victim, in view of the political situation both at Rome and in Asia, though he tried to protect the aged bishop from his folly. Because of the pestilence, and the religious enthusiasm which followed it, no other solution was possible.

We must notice that in the procedure of Polycarp's investigation a new element has come in. It is the loyalty oath. Such oaths were common in Oriental kingdoms and were used in the Roman empire; we have examples on stone from the reigns of Augustus and Caligula. One from the reign of Caligula reads as follows: "We swear by Zeus the Savior [Jupiter Capitolinus] and by the divine Caesar Augustus and by the native pure Virgin [Athena] that we will be loyal to

Gaius Caesar Augustus and to his whole family, and that we will consider friends those whom he chooses and enemies those whom he rejects. If we keep our oath, may it be well for us; if we break it, the opposite." Such an oath is what the proconsul wanted Polycarp to take. It is a substitute for offering sacrifices to the emperor's image, a practice which Pliny used but which the emperor Trajan did not encourage. Those who took the oath offered sacrifices to Jupiter Capitolinus, just as Christians were expected to take the oath and sacrifice.

We can prove that this was the kind of oath involved from the fact that the police officers asked Polycarp to say, "Caesar is Lord," as well as to offer sacrifice. The two items are closely bound together. The proconsul saw that Polycarp was not going to sacrifice, and he therefore tried to strengthen the oath by asking him to curse Christ, as Pliny had earlier done. But since the early Christian tradition did not permit the taking of oaths (Matthew 5, 34) under any circumstances (James 5, 12), Polycarp could not be released.

Under both Marcus Aurelius and his son, the loyalty oath played a significant part in Christian cases. Christians were willing to pray for the emperor, but they would not take oaths or offer sacrifices, since in their view (and that of many philosophers) God needs no sacrifices. After all, they had broken with Judaism on the issue of the Jewish law and its sacrifices. They could not accept any others.

With this persecution the plague gradually came to an end. Other Christians were sent to work in the mines, but we know of no further executions.

Five years later the military situation took a turn for the worse. Barbarians broke through the defenses of the empire and even devastated Eleusis near Athens. Both the western and eastern frontiers were endangered. Just at this time the Christian problem became acute again.

Within Christianity there arose a movement led by visionaries who predicted the imminent end of the world and the descent of the New Jerusalem from heaven to a plain between two obscure villages in Phrygia. The prophet Montanus, perhaps an ex-priest of the Great Mother, was accustomed to go into trances and deliver oracles to his disciples. Two prophetesses also possessed this gift. They made much of the Apocalypse of John.

Many followers joined the triad, and they accepted the doctrines of community property, severe asceticism, and watchful waiting. After Montanus and one of the prophetesses died, the survivor, Maximilla, stated to the faithful that she was persecuted as if she were a wolf. She was not really a wolf, she added; she was Word, Spirit, and Power.

Various orthodox writers replied to the prophet, but for the moment it was impossible to be sure he was wrong. Even after 180 Irenaeus could not absolutely reject Montanism. The Roman church remained in doubt. Under these circumstances, Roman officials must have found it difficult to separate Montanism from Christianity, although in Asia, where Montanists were often eager for martyrdom, various Christian bishops denounced the movement. The prophetess Maximilla died in 179 still predicting wars and revolutions before the end would come.

There were certainly Christians who were loyal to the Roman state. Many of these were enlisted in the twelfth legion (*Legio Fulminata*), stationed in Cappadocia as part of the eastern defense system. And a test of their loyalty was provided in the year 175, when Avidius Cassius, governor of Syria, led a revolt against Marcus Aurelius.

This revolt is one of the most peculiar events in Roman history. The empress Faustina apparently despaired of her husband's health and had Avidius informed that the emperor was dying. On receipt of the news, Avidius did not wait for senatorial approval but informed his troops that the emperor had become a god. He proclaimed himself emperor; Cilicia, Judaea, and Egypt joined Syria in supporting him. The twelfth legion barred him from Cappadocia, however. Though he was soon killed—against the emperor's command to spare him—there was a new atmosphere of instability in the empire. The popular Jewish-Christian Sibylline Oracles speak regretfully of Avidius' death and seem to identify Marcus with the "beast" of the Apocalypse of John.

With peace momentarily restored, a Christian bishop in Asia addressed a statement of loyalty to the emperor. He spoke of a miraculous storm which had terrified the Quadi several years earlier, and claimed that it was due to the prayers of the Christian twelfth legion. Its name (*fulminatrix*) had been given it because of this miracle.

What could an imperial secretary make of this document? A sudden storm had in fact resulted in Roman victory. But there were several explanations of its cause. Prayer to the Roman gods was one possibility; the magic of an Egyptian named Arnuphis was another. The emperor seems to have favored Arnuphis, though the evidence of his coins is ambiguous. The name *fulminata* had been borne by the legion since Augustus' day, though *fulminatrix* may well have been a popular title given after the storm. The secretary would probably conclude that Christian claims were somewhat exaggerated. He would wonder what Christians were doing in the twelfth legion.

Meanwhile the emperor had terminated his campaigns. He was aware that in order to secure the East he had to make a personal tour of inspection. With Faustina and the young Commodus, now given the title Leader of the Youth, Marcus set out for the provinces which had aided Avidius Cassius. While passing from Alexandria to Antioch he went through Judaea, where he expressed his contempt for the Jews he saw. Beyond Antioch Faustina died and was deified. Marcus and Commodus spent much time in Asia and finally reached Athens, where they were initiated in the Eleusinian mysteries, in the autumn of 176. Coins of this year speak of "eternal peace."

The aging emperor was obviously trying to make the empire secure for his motherless son, who was only fifteen. Foreign affairs seemed to be under control, and only domestic enemies remained. Marcus' earlier clemency toward supporters of Avidius Cassius was replaced by more severe measures, probably after Faustina's death. He provided that the property of dead rebels should be confiscated, and added that in such cases slaves could be tortured for information about their masters. Furthermore, those who had aided Avidius by religious prophecies were to be banished. Superstition (foreign religion) was discouraged.

Under such circumstances, it was easy for those who wanted the property of Christians to bring charges against them as disloyal. The storm first broke in Asia Minor, after the imperial visit. We first hear of it in an appeal to the emperor made by Melito, bishop of Sardis. He describes the robberies and murders committed by informers, and expresses his optimistic doubts that the new decrees really come from the emperor. He asks for a personal investigation by Marcus Aurelius.

Melito states that the new decree is not fitting even against barbarian enemies. The policy of Marcus Aurelius toward the Marcomanni had often been one of pacification as well as victory; and the king of the Quadi had been punished only by banishment to Alexandria. Melito believes that Christians should be treated at least equally well. Admittedly their philosophy originated among barbarians and first grew among them, but it flourished within the empire in the reign of Augustus, and the Roman empire developed along with it. Later emperors honored it along with other religions. Only Nero and Domitian, now universally criticized, wished to attack it.

Melito argues that what is good for the Christian church is good for the Roman empire. Christianity is no more a novelty than the empire itself. The real novelty in the present crisis is the persecution of the godly. This persecution is unjust and cannot have been decreed by a just emperor, whose commands Christians gladly obey.

Christianity is a philosophy which exists for the good of the empire. After its rise the empire prospered in accordance with the prayers of all men. We do not know how Melito developed this theme in the lost portions of his apology, but he probably argued that imperial acceptance and advocacy of Christianity would bring even greater prosperity and glory. He certainly says that Marcus Aurelius became the prayed-for heir of the empire and that he would rule with his son, if he guarded the philosophy which was brought up with the empire and began with Augustus.

The tension between church and state is ascribed to misunderstanding on the part of the state. This analysis is probably due to Melito's treatment of Christianity as philosophy. If the emperor knew the good he would do the good. Melito does not mention the obvious fact that in Trajan's rescript the punishment of Christians as Christians is taken for granted. He looks only on the moderating rescripts of Hadrian and Antoninus Pius, and assumes that Marcus Aurelius holds the same view, "although far more humanely and philosophically." His conclusion is that "we are confident that you will do everything we ask."

In Melito's words we hear the voice of the rich and self-confident churches of Asia Minor. A decade earlier, Sagaris of Laodicea had been martyred, as Melito well knew; but he did not feel he could mention this fact after so long a period of tranquillity.

What kind of response can his *Apology* have received at Rome? When the imperial secretary examined it, he must have been quite aware that it was unacceptable both on religious and on historical grounds. First, religious: obviously this philosophy had not been responsible for the development of Roman power, since it denied the existence and the power of the Roman gods. Second, historical: neither Nero nor Domitian, bad as they were, had persecuted Christians except as criminals or tax evaders, and it had arisen not under Augustus but under Tiberius. Moreover, neither Hadrian nor Antoninus Pius had modified the anti-Christian legislation of Trajan; they had simply regularized procedure and prevented action due to mob psychology. The only recognizable point in Melito's appeal lay in his complaint about disorder in Asia Minor. This could be corrected, although the manner of correction would have to depend on the circumstances. The imperial secretary would conclude that the Christian bishop was drawing an exaggerated picture, although his protestation of loyalty sounded fairly sincere. The expression "our philosophy" would annoy the emperor, and the *Life* of Marcus tells us that "it was said that under the guise of philosophy certain persons were vexing both the state and private persons—the emperor removed this."

Other Oriental religions eagerly expressed their loyalty to the emperor and to his son. This was notably true of the worshipers of the Syrian Jupiter Heliopolitanus, since the rebel Avidius Cassius had been strongly supported in Syria. In December 176 a great basilica was begun on the Janiculum for this god, and we possess the dedicatory inscription. It reads "For the safety and return and victory of the emperors Augustus Antoninus and Commodus Caesar, Leader of the Youth, Victor over the Sarmatians." It had been given by a prominent urban official who later placed an inscription at Ostia for the safety of the two emperors, and as late as 186 erected an altar to Jupiter Heliopolitanus. There could be no question about the loyalty of the Syrian god.

At the end of 176 the boy Commodus was made co-emperor with his father.

Early in the year 177 the Athenian Christian Athenagoras began the composition of his *Embassy on Behalf of the Christians*, a work intended to appeal to the emperors by refuting the common charges against Christians. In form and in temper it is different from the *Apology* of Justin; it is logically coherent and its mood is irenic. It is addressed to "the emperors Marcus Aurelius Antoninus and Lucius Aurelius Commodus, victors over the Armenians and the Sarmatians, but most important, philosophers."

Your world, greatest of kings, uses various customs and laws, and no one is compelled by law or fear of punishment not to love his ancestral ways, even if they are ridiculous.

After citing various examples of religious toleration, Athenagoras claims that the Christians are hated simply because of their name and without any examination. This situation should be changed:

Admiring your gentleness and benignity and your irenic and humane attitude toward all, individuals enjoy equity and cities share equal honors in proportion to their importance; the whole world enjoys profound peace because of your wisdom.

Only Christians are unjustly deprived not only of their property but of life itself:

It is your task, great, humane and most learned kings, to remove the abuse which we suffer by law so that, as the whole world shares in your benefactions both individually and as cities, we too may have favor with you, proud because we have stopped being the object of informers.

Such an action would be worthy of imperial justice and of emperors who can see this all the more clearly since they are philosophers and eager for all learning.

Athenagoras' attitude is not unprecedented. Probably many Christians still believed that the tension between empire and church could find a peaceful resolution. He ends his *Embassy* on the same note:

You, who in every respect by nature and by education are completely good (*chrestoi*) and moderate and humane and worthy of ruling, should incline your royal head to me now that I have destroyed the accusations and have proved that we are religious, moral, and chastened in soul. For who are more worthy of obtaining what they ask for than we are, who pray for your rule that—as is most just—you may receive the empire in succession, son from father, and that your rule may receive increase and addition, with all men your subjects? And this is to our own advantage, "so that we may lead a quiet and peaceable life" [1 Tim. 2, 2] and readily obey all the ordinances.

The tone, almost of adulation, with which Athenagoras addresses the emperors, is in part explained by a singular passage in which Marcus Aurelius and Commodus are compared with God and the Logos, the Son of God, and it is stated that the emperors received the empire "from above." This expression is apparently based on John 19, 11, where Jesus tells Pilate that Roman power would not exist were it not "from above."

We have already seen that Justin found some meaning in the fact that Jewish rule in Judaea came to an end at the time of the birth of Jesus, and that Melito went on to find meaning in the fact that the Roman empire began then. This idea can be traced back to the opening chapters of the gospel of Luke. Among the apologists Athenagoras goes farther, however, when he develops the Roman doctrine of the divine appointment of rulers, set forth by Paul in Romans 13 and by Clement of Rome at the end of his letter to the Corinthians.

What Athenagoras complains about is primarily the robbing of Christians by informers and others. People generally regarded the Christians as guilty of godlessness, cannibalism, and incest. The first charge is clearly based on their refusal to offer sacrifices to the images of the gods: Athenagoras answers it by attacking both images and sacrifice. He then takes up the charge of incest, refuting it by a description of Christian morality. He claims that real cannibalism is found not among Christians but among those who persecute them. The persecutors are breaking both the laws now in effect and the

FORSYTH LIBRARY
FORT HAYS KANSAS STATE COLLEGE

precedents set by previous emperors. They engage in mob action which goes beyond the decisions of provincial governors. Athenagoras concludes his work with a promise to prove the rationality of resurrection, an appeal to the virtues of the emperors, and a promise of Christian loyalty to Commodus.

Athenagoras' appeal might have had some effect if the "deep peace" which he mentions had lasted. Unfortunately, in the spring of 177 war broke out again, even though the two emperors tried to preserve public calm by remaining at Rome until the following year.

The people were weary of wars and eager to find scapegoats, now that external peace had proved to be temporary. In the summer of 177 mob violence broke out in two cities of Gaul. The center of the crisis was Lyons, the religious center of the province. This was the seat of the provincial council and the city of the great temple of Augustus, first built in 12 B.C. and later restored by Antoninus Pius. The dedication day, August 1, was one of the great festivals of the province.

Lyons was also a Christian center. Many gnostics had come there, with their questionable rites of sacred marriage; many Montanists had also come, bringing their predictions of war and revolution. The mob attacked the Christians' property and their persons. They accused them not only of being Christians, but also of practising incest, cannibalism, and sexual aberrations. To complete the picture, they claimed that Christians were both godless and irrational. The Christians involved were imprisoned for their own protection.

Unfortunately, when the proconsul of Gaul came on the scene he followed the new regulations of Marcus Aurelius and ordered a general search made for Christians; he then tortured the slaves of Christian masters. In order to clear themselves, some of these slaves confirmed the suspicions of the mob. Even those in Lyons who had not been unfriendly toward Christians became hostile. The governor managed to delay the execution of Roman citizens by writing to Marcus Aurelius, but when the rescript came it simply reiterated Trajan's regulation: "They are to be beheaded, but those who recant are to be released." Since the games were at hand, at the beginning of August, the Roman citizens were beheaded and the rest sent to the wild beasts. Some had been fortunate enough to suffocate in prison, and one Roman citizen went to the beasts because he had aroused the mob's anger. As a special mark of the governor's disfavor, the bodies of the martyrs were refused burial and kept in the open air for six days. Then they were burned to ashes and thrown into the river Rhone.

Clearly this case, though it had begun with mob action, was intended as an example to other Christians. The emperor himself had been consulted about the proceedings, and he had approved the execution of Roman citizens. If the Christians would come to their senses and abandon their superstition, they could join in the defense of the world empire. Otherwise they would be hunted down as self-condemned criminals. We shall see that Celsus offers them this choice. The emperor had to set his house in order before leaving it to his son. Considerations of internal security had become paramount.

The surviving Christians of Lyons and Vienne sent circular letters to the Christian communities throughout the world. They described the martyrdoms and pointed to the endurance of the saints. We can only imagine the shock with which Melito and Athenagoras must have read their descriptions. Their loyalty must have been shaken. From their silence, and from the silence of Eleutherus of Rome and Theophilus of Antioch, we can conclude that these influential leaders did not wish to stir up further troubles by publicly praising the martyrs. They must have hoped to ride out the gale with as little damage as possible.

The Christians of Lyons also wrote Eleutherus to condemn the activities of Montanists. Probably the apocalyptic enthusiasm of Montanist fanatics had had something to do with the hatred of the mob. The Montanist prophets had predicted further wars and revolutions. Doubtless they pointed to the resumption of warfare as fulfillment of their prophecies. The Christians of Gaul wanted to dissociate themselves from these disloyal elements.

In the Orient, however, a voice was raised which must have shocked pagans and Christians alike. This was the voice of the Syrian Tatian. A dozen years before, he had been a disciple of Justin at

Rome and with Justin had been bitterly attacked by the Cynic Crescens, who had the ear of certain Roman officials and brought both Justin and Tatian to their attention. After Justin's death, Tatian had returned to his native Syria, and in his reaction from Justin's mediating Christianity had turned to extreme asceticism. He had come to deny the goodness of the created world, to insist upon the weakness of the Creator, and to hold that marriage, a form of fornication, was inspired by Satan. Most men had lost the divine spirit which alone could give immortality to the human soul. Christ, "the god who suffered," had come to redeem mankind, but he was not a human being descended from David. In order to propagate these views Tatian had composed a harmony of the gospels, his famous *Diatessaron*, and had written a book of *Problems* dealing with the inconsistencies of the Bible, as well as a treatise *On Animals*, in which he argued that apart from the divine spirit men and animals are essentially the same.

Because of this theological position Tatian's support was not especially welcome, and the attitude toward the state and toward Graeco-Roman culture set forth in his *Address to the Greeks* could only confirm the worst suspicions of imperial authorities. The *Address* is a bitter, distorted, powerful hymn of hate directed against the philosophy, religion, science, and art of the Graeco-Roman world. It is written by a man who claims to have passed through all the fields of learning he now rejects, a man who, born a barbarian, has learned to value barbarism above civilization. He piles slander on denunciation. The only positive note he strikes is at the end of his work, where (relying on Hellenistic Jewish sources) he proceeds to demonstrate the chronological priority of Moses to all Greek learning. His style is at once rhetorical and obscure, and he employs unusual words to prove the worthlessness of the rhetoric he employs.

Tatian does not refuse to pay taxes to the Roman emperor, or to serve him, though he calls such service slavery; but he will fear God alone and give only human honor to a human king. He would rather die than deny God. His soul is free from "the slavery in the world," and he despises rulers and tyrants. He states that he will not be an officer in the Roman army. He despises Greek and Roman legislation with its contradictions; there ought to be one law and one common state. The construction of the world is good, but its political structure is evil. Tatian denounces the emperor's endowment of philosophical schools at Athens, and claims that cannibalism and incest are Greek, not Christian.

Tatian's tactlessness is obvious in his mention of the deification of Antinous, the favorite of Hadrian.

How was the dead Antinous, a beautiful youth, set in the moon? Who made him ascend?—unless perhaps as men, perjuring themselves for payment, are believed when they say (ridiculing the gods) that kings have ascended into heaven, so someone has similarly called him a god and has been deemed worthy of honor and reward.

A regular feature of the Roman consecration of royal persons was the oath taken by some official to establish the ascension of the person concerned, and the payment of a fee for the oath. When Justin mentioned the oath his reference did not need to be taken so seriously. But Tatian was writing soon after the death and deification of the empress Faustina. Her ascension is represented on the triumphal arch of Marcus Aurelius.

In addition to the other difficulties presented by Tatian's address, there is the fact noticed by Wilamowitz that in the eighteenth chapter Tatian seems to be describing some well known person in these words:

Those who are considered gods, invading the bodies of certain persons and producing a sense of their presence by dreams, command them to come forth into public, and in the sight of all, when they have taken their fill of the things of this world, fly away from the sick and destroying the disease which they had produced, restore men to their former state.

The "certain persons" may well be one person, the famous rhetorician Aelius Aristides of Smyrna, who began the publication of his *Sacred Discourses* describing his healing by the gods through dreams in the year 175. In Aristides, Tatian chose an unfortunate object of attack, for he was a friend of the emperor and obtained imperial gifts for the rebuilding of Smyrna after an earthquake in 178. Tatian also criticized him for affecting Attic Greek while living in Asia Minor!

Thus in his relatively brief address Tatian was able to annoy nearly every potential opponent he might have aroused. It is no wonder that, writing shortly afterward, Irenaeus of Lyons states clearly and emphatically that while Tatian was a Christian during the lifetime of his teacher Justin, he is now a purely individual teacher; he is speaking for himself alone and for his misguided pupils.

Tatian's address was also attacked by Aelius Aristides himself, in his forty-sixth oration of about 180. Some Cynic writers, he says, somehow dissociate themselves from the Greeks. They assume the name of philosophers. They do not honor the gods. They do not take part in government. They do not recognize their superiors. They are like "the irreligious men in Palestine." Aristides clearly has Tatian in mind.

Another reply was made by a Platonist philosopher named Celsus, who wrote his *True Account* as apologetic against the Christians. It is not primarily a political work, but it ends with a discussion of political matters, an appeal to Christians to participate in affairs of state. The Christians should not hesitate to take an oath by the emperor, for to him earthly affairs have been given and from him men receive whatever they obtain. There must be one ruler. Otherwise governing would be taken over "by the most lawless and uncivilized barbarians."

Apparently Celsus has heard rather simple Christians say that if the Romans became Christians, God would be the only defender they needed. Does he have in mind the apology of Apollinaris, with its reference to the miraculous victory of the praying legion? He argues that God has hardly defended the Jews, and that Christians are even now being sought for under penalty of death.

Other Christians have suggested that if the emperors were to be converted and this conversion were to affect all men, there could be a single rule and a single law, not only for the Roman empire but even for the whole world. Celsus doubts the possibility of such a universal law. Some modern scholars have doubted that Christians made any such suggestion. But we have seen that Melito seems to suggest that Christianity ought to be the official "philosophy" of the Roman empire, and even Tatian, like Marcus Aurelius, believes that there should be one system of law. Christian leaders before 177 thought that there was a genuine possibility of reconciliation with a state governed by a philosopher-king.

Celsus concludes with an appeal to the loyalty of Christians, an appeal which as we have seen may have met a ready though short-lived response in Asia Minor and at Athens:

It becomes you to ward off every weakness from the emperor and to suffer with him for just causes and to fight for him and be a soldier with him, if necessary, and to wage war and rule for the fatherland, if need be, and to do this for the preservation of the laws and of religion.

Apollinaris, Melito, and Athenagoras had stressed the loyalty of Christians to the emperors and the empire. Celsus calls on them to act upon their profession, to live as well as speak as Romans. It might have been expected that Christians would respond to his appeal. Unfortunately, the actions of the Roman state spoke more loudly than its avowals of justice. The martyrdoms at Lyons ended any possibility of a rapprochement between church and state at least within the second century.

On the other hand, the court physician Galen mentions Christians several times in works written between 177 and 180. He criticizes the traditionalism and irrationality both of Jews and of Christians but praises their contempt of death, their self-discipline, and their pursuit of justice. As Walzer says, "Galen is the first Greek philosopher in Rome who, without being a Christian himself, gave a fair and sympathetic appreciation of the Christians for philosophical reasons." We may suppose that his influence was felt in court circles, especially under Commodus.

Marcus Aurelius provides us with a striking example of a ruler who from the highest motives of devotion to the state and its religion strove to defend the empire from its enemies foreign and domestic. Like the proconsul Sergius Paullus and the prefect Rusticus, he was a philosopher. He explicitly states that the Christians died simply because of their obstinacy. Just so, Pliny had written Trajan: "I did not doubt that, whatever they confessed, certainly their stubbornness and inflexible obstinacy ought to be punished." They were subversive because they would not conform to the religio-political constitution of the empire. Their religion was novel and therefore they were undoubtedly guilty of all sorts of crimes. Justin had written the emperor Antoninus Pius, "We are your allies in the cause of peace"; all the apologists had stated that they were accustomed to pray for the emperor and the empire. They did not refuse the payment of taxes. But uniformity rather than unity had come to be the ideal of the Roman state as it began its long descent into anarchy and tyranny.

The crux of the problem can be seen in the deification of the dead emperor or empress, ridiculed by Justin and Tatian. The coins issued by the surviving rulers bear the legend *consecratio*. For the Christian, the ruler of the state is subordinate to God. As Theophilus later expresses it, God has entrusted him with a stewardship. For the Roman, the dead Caesar was one of the gods. True security and felicity were to be found in the service of the omnipotent state. The Christian, on the other hand, was often unwilling to serve a state which confused Caesar with God.

Marcus Aurelius died on March 17, 180, but his policy was carried on and even strengthened by the officials he had appointed. His son and heir Commodus busied himself with his father's deification. He was only nineteen years old, and presumably the work of government was conducted by older and wiser men. One of these men, Vigellius Saturninus, proconsul of Africa, decided to suppress Christianity in his province, and on July 16 six Christians were brought before him.

To Saturninus the main problem seemed to be not the question of sacrifice but that of the loyalty oath. He informed the Christians that they could take advantage of the indulgence of the emperor if they would recant. Their leader Speratus, however, replied that his own emperor was Christ, that he did not recognize the empire of the present age, and that he paid taxes only because he acknowledged his own Lord, the king of kings and emperor of all nations. Obviously Speratus was much influenced by the Apocalypse of John. Another Christian was willing to say, "Honor to Caesar as Caesar, but fear to God." Saturninus was pleased by neither answer, and proceeded to ask for an oath by the Genius of the emperor. He asked again for recantation, and offered the Christians a month's stay for reconsideration. They all refused and were all beheaded. Presumably they were not punished more harshly because they belonged to the upper class of Africa.

A few years later Arrius Antoninus, proconsul of Asia, tried to acquit the Christians brought before him. He ordered a few of them executed and said to the rest, "You wretches, if you wish to die, you have cliffs and nooses." His comment did not make them change their minds.

About the same time, in 184 or 185, a Roman senator named Apollonius was brought before the Senate, perhaps because he was implicated in a conspiracy against Commodus. The urban prefect Perennis, soon to die himself because of a plot against the emperor, conducted the investigation. After Apollonius declared himself a Christian, he was first asked to recant and take the oath by the Genius of the emperor Commodus. When he refused, he was next asked to sacrifice to the gods and to the image of Commodus. Since he remained unconvinced, Perennis hastily offered him a stay of three days for reconsideration, pointing out that the Senate had decreed that "Christians were not to exist." After further discussion and final warnings, Perennis stated, "I wish to release you but I am forced by the decree of the emperor Commodus," and reluctantly ordered his execution.

Apollonius was the last martyr to suffer under Commodus. Since 182 the emperor's mistress had been the Christian Marcia, and as her influence over him and in the court increased she was able to prevent further anti-Christian action. Perhaps about the same time Cincius Severus, who was later *pontifex maximus*, gave a formula for Christians to use so that they might be acquitted. We do not know what this was, but we may suspect that it was the formula Tertullian later mentions, an oath not by the Genius but by the safety of the emperor.

Christians could not take an oath by the Genius of the emperor, for to them a Genius (or Fortune, as it was usually translated in Greek) was no more than a demonic power. Christ had come to destroy the demons, and they could not take oaths by demons. Gradually their original hostility toward oaths of any sort came to be abandoned. Their conflict with Rome was on a religious rather than on an ethical or political matter.

Meanwhile there had been a clear declaration of loyalty by a Syrian Christian leader.

As bishop of Antioch, Theophilus occupied a position of considerable authority and responsibility. He therefore found it necessary to express his views in a more temperate manner than that of Tatian, even though his attitude toward Graeco-Roman culture was ultimately the same as Tatian's.

The occasion for writing the third book is explicitly stated in the fourth chapter:

Godless mouths falsely accuse us, the godly who are called Christians, saying that our wives are the common property of all and indulge in promiscuous intercourse; that further we have intercourse with our own sisters; and that—most godless and cruel of all—we taste human flesh.

With these words Theophilus simply paraphrases the charges against Christians already refuted in the *Embassy* of Athenagoras. If he has read the *Embassy*—and this seems unlikely—he probably feels that it is too philosophical and too complicated for the simpler, more matter-of-fact official audience he hopes to reach. To these charges he adds two more:

People also say that our doctrine has made its way only recently, and that we have nothing to say in proof of the truth of our teaching; our doctrine, they say, is foolishness.

Theophilus therefore proceeds to gather all sorts of materials in order to attack pagan philosophy and religion, to defend Christian morality, and to demonstrate the antiquity of the Christian religion which is based on Moses. This chronology proves that "our doctrine is neither recent nor mythical."

In the third book he does not deal with the question of the Christian and the Roman state, except by repeating the teaching of the divine Word which speaks of submission to powers and authorities and of prayer for them, "so that we may lead a quiet and peaceable

life" (1 Timothy 2, 2). It also teaches Christians to render what is
due to all, honor, fear, taxes, and love (Romans 13, 7–8). Elsewhere
he says—although he may be copying his Roman source—that the
Roman power which made Rome great was given by God. The con-
tinuing persecution of Christians is due (not to Romans but) to
Greeks.

Theophilus' positive statement about the Roman emperor is given
in his first book. The Christian cannot worship the emperor, who is
only a man and was not made to be worshiped but to receive legitimate honor. The emperor has been entrusted with a stewardship
from God. He is like God, for just as God alone is God and alone is
to be worshiped, so the emperor alone is emperor; his subordinates
cannot be called kings. Perhaps Theophilus has in mind the Syrian
revolt of Avidius Cassius:

Honor the emperor by being subject to him and praying for him. For by
doing so you will perform the will of God. For the law of God says, "My
son, honor God and the king, and do not be disobedient to either; for they
will suddenly punish their enemies."

Here Theophilus combines phrases from the Pastoral Epistles, Romans, and 1 Peter 2, 15–17, with an explicit quotation of Proverbs
24, 21–22. He is summarizing biblical teaching on this subject, and
is able to express loyalty to the emperor without extravagance. He
develops no theory of the relation of church to state, but they are
apparently coordinate powers. Christian loyalty is due to both.

Theophilus' declaration may have met some response, though the
response is quite ambiguous. This we find, if we find it, in the eighth
oration of the philosopher-rhetorician Maximus of Tyre, who lec-
tured at Rome in the reign of Commodus. In this oration he asked a
hypothetical question:

If we were to provide legislation for any other men, who had just originated from earth outside the ether we know, or had been shaped by some
Prometheus, and lacked experience of human life and law and reason, we
should probably be involved in this problem: should such a race abandon
physical images and worship not ivory or gold or oak or cedar or a river
or a bird, but the rising sun and the shining moon and the variegated
heaven, and earth and air and fire and water? Or should we force them to
the necessity of honoring objects of wood or stone, or images?

Maximus went on in his usual inconclusive way to suggest that if such is the common law for all men, image worship should be enforced, even though it makes no difference how various peoples worship, know, and love the incomprehensible God, provided that they do so.

It seems likely that he had Christians in mind, since they regarded themselves as a "new race," criticized the worship of images, and accused pagans of worshiping the elements. At the same time their opponents often believed that both Jews and Christians worshiped the heaven or the sun. Here Maximus was probably, with great discretion, speaking in favor of tolerating Christianity. After all, some Christians were powerful at Rome.

In any event, after 189 Marcia was strong enough to intervene in favor of Christians who had been condemned to the mines of Sardinia, and she was aided not only by a slave named Proculus but also by the court chamberlain Prosenes. In this period Commodus was busy with his warfare against the Senate, and was searching for supernatural protection, especially that provided by Serapis and Isis. After a disastrous fire at Rome he planned to rebuild the city and name it after the Roman Hercules, with whom he identified himself. The old colossus of Nero was remodeled as Hercules with Commodus' features. And he made plans to execute many senators and appear in the arena on the first day of 193 as both consul and gladiator. The day before, however, Marcia and her allies gave him poison. When it failed to take effect, an athlete with whom he often wrestled strangled him in his bath.

The Senate immediately voted his condemnation, with the comment that he had been more savage than Domitian and more impure than Nero. It is a sad comment on the cycles of power in the Roman empire that good emperors were almost always succeeded by bad ones, who were often too young for their high office. Tiberius was followed by Caligula, Claudius by Nero, Vespasian and Titus by Domitian, Marcus Aurelius by Commodus. Irresponsible power corrupts.

In the last years of Commodus the religious struggle was not so much between Christians and the empire as between the emperor and the empire. In this way the reign of Commodus foreshadows much of the development in the third century. One of the many tragedies of Roman history lies in the almost unintentional revolt of Avidius Cassius in 175. It was he who could have been chosen by Marcus Aurelius as his successor. After his death, which the emperor tried to prevent, the only successor apparently available was the boy Commodus, who as Dio says ended the golden age and brought a new age of iron.

As far as Christianity was concerned, however, the weakness and insanity of Commodus brought greater freedom than the piety and philosophy of Marcus Aurelius. Their basic difficulty lay in the decision of Trajan to root out Christianity, and in the means of testing it provided by sacrifice to Roman gods (sometimes, but not often, including the living emperor) and the loyalty oath. They could accept neither of these tests, even though the overwhelming majority of Christians was loyal to the Roman government. Another century of intermittent persecution was to be required before Rome could recognize religious freedom and distinguish between the Roman religion and the Roman state.

5 Restoration and Reform

AFTER THE MURDER OF COMMODUS THERE FOLLOWED FOUR YEARS OF savage warfare, in which Septimius Severus had to establish his rule against the powerful armies of the governor of Syria, Pescennius Niger, and the governor of Britain, Clodius Albinus. Finally, after four years of desperate fighting, Severus vanquished his enemies and returned to Rome in triumph. As early as 193 the Senate had recognized his ability by proclaiming him emperor. At long last he justified their confidence. Before consolidating his power, Severus had to besiege and finally destroy Byzantium (later Constantinople, now Istanbul), but by the autumn of 196 his troops had occupied it. As the troops of Severus entered the city, Niger's governor Caecilius

Capella exclaimed, "Christians, rejoice!" His outburst suggests that Christians were not entirely aloof from politics.

In 197 the former lawyer, now Christian, Tertullian addressed a powerful apology to the governors of Roman provinces. Of all the Christian apologies this one is the most direct and to the point. Tertullian has just written two books *To the Nations*, based largely on Varro, in which he argued for Christianity on the basis of Varro's theology. Now he revises his previous work and makes it politically relevant. After a lengthy introduction on the injustice of accusations against Christians, based on ignorance as their condemnation was based on inconsistency, as in the case of Trajan, he turns to refute the charges brought against them. First he refutes the general charges by turning them back against the accusers. Then he proceeds to develop the real problems. "You do not worship the gods and you do not offer sacrifices for the emperors." In contrast to the deified dead men of Roman religion Tertullian develops the reality of Christian faith. Then he argues that ordinarily provincials are free to worship their own gods. While some say that the empire is due to the piety of the Romans, actually it is due to the power of the one God. Christians are not guilty of offending deities who do not really exist. Finally he comes to the question of sacrifices for the emperor. Actually his so-called Genius is a demon, and angels, demons, and gods, are really inferior to the emperor himself. Christians pray for him, as the Christian books prove. Furthermore, Christians pray for a delay to the end of the Roman empire since they recognize that something far worse will come after it. They can take oaths not by the emperor's (demonic) Genius but by his safety, which is more "august."

The emperor has been chosen by God (after hard fighting, Tertullian might have said), but he is not God. Christians can call him Lord in the ordinary way, but not if they are forced to do so. After all, Augustus himself, as Tertullian well knows from Suetonius, refused to use the title. Moreover, Christians are in fact rather than in theory loyal. They did not support Avidius Cassius, Niger, or Albinus. On the other hand, if they were really disloyal they would be the most dangerous enemies the empire has ever known. Their sheer force of numbers could make the empire collapse. Therefore they should be classified among legitimate sects and not considered illegal.

Tertullian's profession of loyalty was not unique; we possess an inscription which praises Severus for restoring the republic and the power of the Roman people. His triumph over anarchy met a widespread response. When he was on his expedition against the Parthians in the East in early 197, even non-Christian observers in Judaea witnessed a remarkable meteorological phenomenon. For forty days a fortified city appeared before dawn, though when the sun rose it vanished. Christians were sure that this was the heavenly Jerusalem, long promised by the Apocalypse of John, and now arriving in Severus' reign.

On the other hand, Tertullian enthusiastically recommended the destruction of supporters of Severus' rivals who consulted astrologers and other soothsayers, and this advice, no doubt proffered by others, was followed. Severus actually put to death many who had consulted Chaldaeans or soothsayers concerning his safety. Unfortunately, during his stay in the East he came to believe that the enthusiasm of Jews and Christians was equally dangerous for the future, and he published a decree in 201 forbidding either Jews or Christians to make converts. Perhaps the decree was in part designed to protect the emperor's infant son, Caracalla, whose nurse, as Tertullian's treatise *To Scapula* points out, was a Christian.

Tertullian's *Apology*, though it did not achieve its purpose, is one of the greatest monuments of early Christian literature. Tertullian's harsh sarcasm, his biting turn of phrase, his obscure style—all these made his work a magnificent work of art, as well as an instrument which could only annoy rather than convince Roman authorities.

As a result of Severus' legislation Christians came to be investigated once more, beginning in 203. The scene of their persecution was Africa and Alexandria. The charge brought against them was not based on the new decree of Severus but on the old law which had simply denied Christians the right to exist. Tertullian himself was probably the author of the *Martyrdom of Perpetua and Felicity*, the earliest notice of the conflict. Beautifully and compellingly written, it describes the innocence and the suffering of the victims. For our purposes, however, we need consider only the questions addressed by Hilarianus, a Roman procurator, to the young woman Perpetua. He instructed her to have pity on the old age of her father and the infancy of her son by offering a sacrifice for the safety of the emperor. This was as far as Hilarianus could go in exercising leniency toward the Christians. He did not require an oath; he simply asked for a sacrifice for the emperor's safety. He had been led to believe that this formula was acceptable to Christians. It was not acceptable, however, for Christians firmly rejected sacrifices of every sort. Perpetua refused. Only at this point did Hilarianus ask her if she were a Christian. When she said she was, her condemnation was inevitable. She was condemned to the wild animals. Some enthusiastic pagans at Carthage proposed that her male companions be dressed as priests of the local Saturn-Baal, and the women as priestesses of the local Ceres, but a Roman tribune refused to permit this procedure. The death penalty was required, however.

In Syria, perhaps aroused by the advent of the heavenly Jerusalem, a bishop persuaded many Christians, men, women, and children, that the end was at hand and that they should go to meet Christ in the desert. The wanderers got lost and were almost arrested and executed by the governor of Syria as a band of robbers. Fortunately for them, the governor's wife was a Christian, and he had the Christians brought back without further penalty. As Hippolytus says, he was trying to avoid a general persecution.

In Pontus another bishop began to see visions and dream dreams. After his third dream he decided that he was a prophet, and informed his flock that within a year the last judgment would take place. The result was a period of incessant prayer; his followers left their employment and most of them sold all their possessions. The bishop began to feel certain doubts about his own accuracy, and informed them that if his predictions were not fulfilled they should no longer believe the scriptures; they should live as they pleased. At the end of the year they mistrusted not the scriptures but the bishop. All were scandalized; the virgins married husbands and the men returned to their farming. Those who had sold out (and presumably had given their funds to the bishop) were compelled to beg.

Hippolytus himself, writing about 203, explained to Roman Christians, apparently not afflicted by persecution, that no one could possibly predict the end of the world, although it would certainly not come for another three hundred years.

At Alexandria, too, probably because the city had become a center of Christian missionary activity, there were outbursts of violence, though it is difficult to tell whether the police spent more time arresting Christians or protecting them from mob attacks. In this persecution the father of the theologian Origen lost his life, but the number of martyrs does not seem to have been great. At this point a certain Judas produced a treatise in which he studied the prophecies of Daniel and concluded (against Hippolytus) that the end of the world was near.

After this short wave of persecution, there came a period of tranquillity. Tertullian tells us of the Roman governor Servilius Pudens, who in about 210 tore up an accusation against a Christian and dismissed him on the ground that his accuser had not appeared. Presumably Pudens had the old rescript of Hadrian in mind.

In 211, the year in which Septimius Severus died while with his army in Britain, Tertullian produced a treatise *On the Military Crown* in which he advocated absolute pacifism. It may be said that such an attitude was doubtless easier for a civilian to hold than for a soldier. And Grégoire may well be right in suggesting that Tertullian's treatise provoked a counterattack by Julius Scapula, proconsul of Africa. Tertullian replied with another pamphlet. In this he argued that religion cannot be forced but must come spontaneously, and that the supreme God has no need of the sacrifices which Roman authorities want to offer. He pointed out that Christians had not joined the revolts of Avidius Cassius, Albinus, or Niger (as he had said already in his *Apology*), and traced the misfortunes, due to divine displeasure, of those governors who persecuted Christians. With these persecutors he contrasted the governors who had helped Christians escape and pointed to the semi-Christian household of Septimius Severus himself.

The relevance of Tertullian's writing was sharply diminished in the year he wrote, for in 212 the new emperor Caracalla extended Roman citizenship to all inhabitants of the empire, presumably (as Dio says) in order to enlarge the base of taxation. At the same time all the gods of the empire were finally admitted within the *pomerium* at Rome, and Caracalla erected a temple of Serapis on the Quirinal. He took part in the Egyptian rites and went so far as to wear the jackal's head of Anubis. In this fact we see the final result of popular pressure. Two and a half centuries earlier Volusius had worn it to escape from the triumvirs. Now the emperor himself acknowledged the power of the gods of Egypt. The rites once Egyptian had become Roman, and Rome, as Ammianus Marcellinus later says, had become "the temple of the whole world." The Egyptian religion, along with other foreign cults, had become the state religion of the empire.

In the reign of Caracalla the celebrated lawyer Domitius Ulpianus wrote ten books *On the Office of the Proconsul*. These were intended to guide the governors of provinces in the performance of their duties, and presumably to take account of the new problems presented by the extension of citizenship. The seventh, eighth, and ninth books were concerned with crime and punishment in the provinces, and in the seventh book, as we learn from Lactantius, there was a collection of imperial rescripts dealing with the Christians. How many foolish papyrus letters would we not sacrifice in exchange for Ulpian's seventh book! Unfortunately we do not have it, and a learned guess that Christians were to be handled in relation to political subversiveness is no substitute.

Such a collection was necessary for several reasons. First, the policy of the emperors toward the church had been moderated. There were no persecutions under Caracalla or his successor Alexander Severus, who is said to have had a statue of Christ in the imperial chapel. Second, Christian forgers had been active in creating imperial edicts. Tertullian's *Apology* contains references to a supposed edict of Marcus Aurelius which recognized the power of Christian prayer against the barbarians and to an edict of Antoninus Pius providing that informers should be burned alive. Since Marcus

Aurelius actually did no more than reiterate the views of Trajan, and since Antoninus Pius did not really favor Christians to such an extent, a collection of authentic rescripts had to be made. Presumably Ulpian used the imperial archives for his researches, since at some point in his career he was imperial secretary.

His book presumably provided the ultimate legal basis for the later persecutions, but in the time in which he wrote its value was largely historical.

The Christians, while doubtless in favor of tolerance for themselves, were not enthusiastic about these superstitions. Tertullian had already seen the hand of God in many catastrophes of the year 211, and there was a strong feeling that the end was at hand. Nevertheless, while Tertullian was praying for the end to come (he had now become a Montanist and favored the quick fullfillment of prophecy), other Christians were taking advantage of toleration to gain converts and work on the problems of Christian theology. The old law against Christians was simply not enforced. On the Christian side there were those who tried to promote harmony with the state and diminish apocalyptic foolishness. A learned presbyter of the Roman church named Gaius produced a treatise in which he argued that the fanciful dreams of the Apocalypse of John were the work of a second century heretic named Cerinthus. Others preferred simply to treat the Apocalypse as allegory.

Under these circumstances the Christian church enjoyed peace for nearly twenty-five years. About 216 came the first dated Christian burial inscriptions. After this time we hear of Origen as a famous theologian at Alexandria and Caesarea; the governor of Arabia asked him to visit his province for theological discussion, and either in 218 or in 232 he accepted an invitation from Julia Mammaea, the mother of the emperor Alexander Severus. To this same princess, Hippolytus of Rome dedicated his apologetic treatise *On the Resurrection*. Obviously Christians were being warmed by the sun of imperial favor.

With the accession of Maximinus the Thracian in 235 the situation worsened, however. It was decided that in order to ensure the doubtful solidarity of the empire, especially against the Persians in the East, the old regulations against Christians should be enforced. From this point on the empire passed through one crisis after another. Rostovtzeff holds that there was actually a plot of peasants and soldiers against the urban middle class. Others have argued, relying on ancient historians, that there was a conflict between the army and the Senate. In either case, chaos was the result. In the remainder of the third century there were twenty-six emperors, and only one was not killed. Money lost its purchasing power as the spiral of inflation swept it away.

Purely local circumstances accounted for the first stages of persecution. In Cappadocia fairly severe earthquakes in 235 resulted in a search for scapegoats, and with the support of the local governor Serenianus, Christians were arrested and sometimes condemned. The situation was not critical, however, until a Montanist prophetess, claiming to be from "Jerusalem," aroused Christians against pagans. Then further troubles began. On the upper Rhine the emperor Alexander Severus tried to buy off the barbarians rather than fight them, and the Roman troops, who doubtless regarded the money as unwisely spent, revolted against him. In the fighting, both the emperor and his powerful mother, Julia Mammaea, were killed. The empire had lost its chief; the Christians had lost their protectress.

At this point the two rival bishops of Rome, Pontianus and Hippolytus, were deported, and Origen wrote his *Exhortation to Martyrdom*. It is by no means certain, however, that Christians were actually put to death, and when the boy emperor Gordianus III came to the throne in 238, informers were severely punished and the provincial governors were ordered to suppress all activities not "in accordance with the principles of the age." Both actions were due to the influence of the Senate. During the next decade Christians were safe. Philip the Arabian (244–249) was said to be a Christian himself. He and his wife exchanged letters with Origen.

In 247 Philip celebrated the thousandth anniversary of the founding of Rome, but the following year offered signs that the empire was cracking up. Three new claimants for the throne arose, supported by the armies of Pannonia in the north (where Alexander Severus had been killed), of Cappadocia, and of Syria. Origen recognized that a persecution might well result from this chaos. He decided to produce a complete reply to the old charges made by Celsus, since they were still being advanced against Christians and had never been fully answered. As he said, "It is probable that believers' freedom from anxiety for their lives will come to an end when again those who attack Christianity in every possible way regard the multitude of believers as responsible for the revolt which is so strong at this moment, because they are not being persecuted by the governors as they were formerly." Origen was right. Early in 249 rioting took place at Alexandria against the Christians, and when a new emperor came to the throne he decided to enforce loyalty throughout the empire on its old religious and political basis. This was the Emperor Decius, who in Christian tradition was regarded as a "damnable animal."

Late in 249 or early in 250 Decius issued an edict which provided that every inhabitant of the empire, without exception, should offer sacrifice to the gods. Some freedom of choice was permitted. In one of the acts of the martyrs the non-sacrificing Christian is offered his choice among Apollo, Jupiter, and Juno, and in another he is asked to sacrifice to Diana. The gods involved are Roman gods, however.

Certificates of sacrifice were issued by local commissions, and a good many of these have been found in Egypt. One of the most interesting was issued to a priestess of the crocodile god of Egypt:

> To the commission chosen to superintend the sacrifices. From Aurelia Ammonous, daughter of Mystus, of the Moeris quarter, priestess of the god Petesouchos the Great, the Great, the Ever-Living, and priestess of the gods in the Moeris quarter.
>
> I have sacrificed to the gods all my life and without interruption, and now again, in accordance with the decree and in your presence, I have made sacrifice and poured a libation and partaken of the sacred victims.
>
> I request you to certify this below.

The edict of Decius met with general approval, but Christians were often content to buy a certificate without sacrificing. The result was a deep split within the Christian church. The bishops, most of whom had neither sacrificed nor bought certificates, were scandalized with the behavior of those who had. And since most of the bishops had discreetly withdrawn to safety in exile, their criticisms of certificate buyers were not readily accepted.

There were, however, a few martyrs, including Fabianus, bishop of Rome. At Pergamum the bishop Carpus was burned alive, with two staunch supporters, though not before April of 251, and in May of the same year a certain Maximus, who refused to sacrifice to Diana, was stoned to death at Ephesus. The same proconsul, Flavius Optimus, had to deal with both cases.

The efforts made to obtain recantation are shown in the case of Pionius, tortured and finally executed at Smyrna by the proconsul Julius Proclus Quintilianus in March 250. Pionius and the proconsul engaged in a long debate which ended only with Pionius' death. On the other hand, when Acacius came before Flavius Claudius Marcianus, probably in 251, a long theological discussion ended in the complete bewilderment of the proconsul. He sent Acacius to prison and reported to the emperor. According to the Christian account, Decius burst into laughter on reading the report, transferred Marcianus to Pamphylia, and released Acacius. The result is so unlikely that it may well be true.

Other Christians were tortured but not executed, as the case of Origen proves. His health was broken and he died about 253; but he was not put to death under Decius, any more than most of the martyrs whom Cyprian lists. Dionysius of Alexandria seems to suggest that many more Christians fled than were executed.

6 Persecution and the Persians

UNDER DECIUS' SUCCESSOR VALERIAN (253–260), WHO RULED JOINTLY with Gallienus (253–268), there was a period of calm followed by a storm in 257, when the Persians began to invade the Eastern provinces. Of the first period, Dionysius of Alexandria says: "Not a single one of the emperors before him was so kindly and favorably disposed toward the Christians as he manifestly was, when he received them at the beginning in the most intimate and friendly manner; indeed all his house was filled with godly persons, and was a church of God." But when the Persian crisis began Valerian was advised to return to the old religion, and he followed the advice. His first edict ordered bishops, presbyters, and deacons to sacrifice to the gods and forbade Christian meetings either in churches or in cemeteries.

In accordance with this edict, Dionysius of Alexandria was summoned before Aemilianus, deputy-prefect of Egypt, who offered him the opportunity of recanting. Dionysius argued that "not all men worship all the gods." Each worships the gods he considers real, and therefore Christians worship the one creator-God who gave imperial power to his favorites Valerian and Gallienus. Christians worship him and pray unceasingly for the safety and continuance of the empire. Aemilianus replied:

Who is forbidding you to worship this god, if he is a god, along with the gods who exist by nature? For you were commanded to worship the gods, that is, the gods whom all recognize.

Dionysius refused, and was sent into exile. A similar investigation took place at Carthage and is reported in the *Acts of Cyprian*. Presumably the same pattern was followed everywhere.

This edict resulted in many exiles but it was no more effective than the more severe edict of Decius had been. It was not severe, and apparently it could be disregarded if it was disregarded with discretion. After all, the Christians were a strong, well knit group. They were allied with the middle class whose support the Senate was trying to hold, and there were also many Christians in the army. In Doura on the eastern frontier, a bastion which the Persians had taken in 256, there was not only a shrine of the military Mithras but also a Christian chapel.

In 258, however, Valerian decided to strengthen and reissue his edict. This time he clearly intended to strike at the aristocratic supporters of the church. Christian officials (bishops, presbyters, deacons) were to be executed. As for the laity, those of high rank (senators, equestrians) were to lose their status and their property, and if they persevered as Christians they were to be executed. Women of high rank were to lose their property and go into exile. Even if any of these persons recanted, they could not recover their property, which reverted to the emperor. Ex-slaves of the imperial household, whether they recanted or not, were to lose their property and be sent in chains to the imperial estates.

The first test of this decree was offered by Xystus, bishop of Rome, who with four deacons visited a Christian cemetery, where he was arrested by the police and executed. Another famous martyr was Cyprian of Carthage, who was brought before the proconsul Galerius Maximus:

Are you Thascius Cyprianus?
I am.
Have you set yourself as "pope" over the men of sacrilegious mind?
I have.
The most sacred emperors have ordered you to offer sacrifice.
I refuse.
Consider your situation.
Do what you have been commanded, for in so just a case there can be no consideration.

After consideration with his council, Galerius Maximus issued his verdict. "For a long time you have lived with sacrilegious mind and you have set yourself up as an enemy to the Roman gods and their sacred rites, assembled many men of your nefarious conspiracy; the pious and most sacred emperors Valerian and Gallienus, the Augusti, and Valerianus the most noble Caesar have not been able to recall you to the observance of their rites. Therefore, since you have been apprehended as the author and leader of most iniquitous crimes, you will be an example to those whom you joined with yourself in your crime. Discipline will be sealed by your blood." Cyprian was then beheaded.

The language of the proconsul's decision is archaic. It recalls the persecution under Marcus Aurelius and Commodus, and betrays no realization of the facts of imperial life in the third century. Christians were not conspirators; they were not dangerous to the empire; they were more loyal than most, and their membership was drawn not from the rabble which the government feared but from the highest classes of the state, as Valerian's edict proves. The Roman empire in its extremity looked for scapegoats, since it was unable to provide any stability on its outworn religious and political grounds.

Another victim was Fructuosus, a bishop in Spain, who refused to offer sacrifice and was burned alive in 259 after a brief interrogation. The last question asked Fructuosus was, "Are you a bishop?" He answered, "I am." The proconsul remarked, "You have been," and ordered his execution.

In the next year, however, Valerian was captured by Shapur, king of Persia. After being humiliated by the Persian king, he was killed; his corpse was flayed and placed in a Persian temple in memory of his defeat. There it was often shown to Roman emissaries. This event neither Romans nor Christians could ever forget.

Gallienus received sole authority, and one of his first acts was to rescind the edict against the Christians. Once more toleration had come to the church.

> The emperor Caesar Puplius Licinius Gallienus Pius Fortunatus Augustus to Dionysius [either of Alexandria or of Rome] and Pinnas and Demetrius and the other bishops.
> I have ordered the beneficence of my pardon to be confirmed throughout the world, so that they may withdraw from the places of worship, and so that by this means you may be able to use a copy of my decree, so that no one may trouble you.

The chancellor of the exchequer was instructed to carry out this decision, and another edict to the bishops allowed them to recover the cemeteries. The ownership of property was thus permitted for the Christian church, as it apparently had been in the early days of the third century, and full freedom was finally given to the practice of Christianity.

Gallienus' successor Aurelian actually intervened in the deposition of Paul of Samosata, bishop of Antioch, but his basic reason was not concern with church affairs but Paul's close association with Zenobia, queen of Palmyra, an enemy of Rome. It is worth noting, however, that no hint is given of a persecution because of Christian political activity. Rome struck at the individual rather than at the group. It was said that Aurelian planned to issue edicts against Christians, but in any case he died in 275 before signing them.

Another quarter-century followed in which the church lived in peace. To be sure, the Neoplatonist philosopher Porphyry wrote fifteen bitter books against the Christians, criticizing nearly every element in the Bible and in the theology of the church. But there is no reason to suppose that at the time his books influenced official policy in any way.

The only religion officially suppressed during the early years of Diocletian and Galerius, who finally triumphed over the Persians in the year 296, was Manichaeism, the heir of Oriental gnosticism. Protected by one Persian king, Mani had been executed by another; but his religion was spreading throughout the East. Diocletian could see no reason to accept Persian religion while crushing Persian power. Probably in 296 he sent a rescript to the proconsul of Africa, instructing him to burn the leaders of the Manichaean movement and behead or imprison their followers. Their property was to be confiscated. Their books were to be burned. They were following "a new and unheard-of monster, which has come to us from the Persians, a hostile people, and has perpetrated many misdeeds." Christians presumably were not averse to this action, though only one later Christian writer mentions it. They did not see that the sword taken up against the Manichaeans could just as readily be turned against themselves.

7 The Sword and the Cross

AFTER THIS PERIOD OF RESPITE WE COME TO THE LAST GREAT EFFORT OF the Roman state to suppress Christianity. It was an abysmal failure. Had such an effort been made two hundred years earlier it might conceivably have been successful, but at the time of the last persecution the occasion for it had passed. One can only marvel at the administrative ineptitude of the officials who proposed it and carried it through. In trying to restore the old religious foundation of Rome they were building with sand on sand.

They were building with sand because the basic problems had nothing to do with the old Roman religion. The disasters of seventy years, to some extent checked under Diocletian, had resulted in the gravest kind of economic and political problems. The famous edict of Diocletian in 301 was an attempt to solve the economic problem by rigorous and unworkable price control. The fire at the palace in Nicomedia, which was said to be the work of Christians, recalls nothing so much as the Reichstag fire of 1933. To the emperors, and by now there were four at the same time, the solution to Rome's troubles seemed to be absolute dictatorship, the creation of a totalitarian state.

The emperor to whom the religious solution appeared most useful was Galerius. Early in 303 the augurs at the palace in Nicomedia (Bithynia) were examining livers, and their efforts were thwarted by Christians in the palace guard who crossed themselves to drive away demons. Both Diocletian and Galerius were present, and Galerius, urged on by his superstitious mother, pointed out to Diocletian the unfortunate effect of Christian exorcism. Aiding him in his anti-Christian activity was a certain Sossianus Hierocles, governor of Bithynia and author of two books against the Christians in which he had brought Celsus' and Porphyry's attacks up to date. After long discussion, in which Diocletian tried to moderate the zeal of Galerius, who wanted the Christians burned alive, an edict was finally issued. Modeled on the second edict of Valerian, it provided that on the feast of the Terminalia (February 23) Christian churches were to be seized and destroyed and the Christian writings were to be burned. Christians were to lose all legal rights and whatever rank they might have, and ex-slaves were to be returned to slavery.

Galerius, however, was not content with this edict, and under his direction a mysterious fire devastated the palace. He immediately claimed that the Christians, public enemies, were trying to burn the emperors alive. Diocletian unfortunately believed his claim, and had an investigation made of the palace guards, without any result. At this point another mysterious fire broke out, and though it was soon put out, Galerius fled, for fear, as he said, that he would be burned alive. The aged Diocletian then proceeded to force his Christian wife and daughter to offer sacrifices, and issued an edict of the sort Galerius had wanted. This second edict was an order for the arrest of all Christian bishops, presbyters, and deacons. As soon as orders could be prepared, a third edict followed which required these Christians to offer sacrifice under penalty of torture and death.

The first execution apparently took place in Palestine on June 7, 303. The governor urged Procopius to sacrifice to the gods. He refused, saying that there was only one God. The governor agreed, and suggested a sacrifice to the four emperors. When Procopius expressed his preference for monarchy (divine or human) he was beheaded. Oddly enough, in Hierocles' treatise against the Christians he too had stated that there was one supreme God, the king, the creator of the universe. The basic conflict between the philosophy and the traditional religion of the empire had led to such an impasse.

Most governors seem to have followed their heads rather than their traditions, and we know of only four martyrs in Palestine during the next two years. There may have been more in Egypt, but Roman relations with Egyptians were never very good.

The reason we hear so little of the Roman church during this period is that Marcellinus, bishop of Rome, who died peacefully in 304, had already demonstrated his loyalty to the state and to the Western emperor Severus by burning incense on a pagan altar and by handing over the Christian scriptures. In the ensuing conflict for the papacy no bishop was chosen until 307, when the new Western emperor Maxentius, who had meanwhile seized power, decided on a policy of toleration. The episcopal election resulted in the victory of the rigorist Marcellus, but there was a militant Christian opposition which preferred to treat sacrificers as Christians. When pitched battles between the two parties took place in Rome, the emperor intervened and banished Marcellus. In April of 308, Maxentius permitted another election, but the new bishop could not reconcile the two parties and was banished to Sicily. His successor was not chosen until after the edict of toleration.

Meanwhile in the East a new edict was issued (in 305); this edict tried to recover the lost spirit of Decius' reign. All inhabitants of the Roman empire were ordered to sacrifice and make libations to the gods. Roman policy was lost in a dream of the past, and these successive edicts give the impression of frantic archaizing.

The number of martyrs was still not very great, although certainly Christians all over the empire were harassed by the police, imprisoned, and sometimes killed. Some of them were so strongly offended by the impiety, not to say stupidity, of the edicts that they attacked their attackers. In 306 the governor of Palestine was offering a libation when a Christian held his arm and would not let him go on. The guards seized him and tortured him unmercifully before his execution. At Alexandria a Christian who had watched Hierocles, now prefect of Egypt, sentencing men to torture and women to prostitution knocked him to the ground and tried to beat him to death. He too became a martyr.

Finally, in 309, a fifth edict was published. This edict recognized the lack of positive elements in the preceding four and attempted to fill the vacuum with, of all things, a restoration of the old Roman religion. The edict sounds like the ages of Augustus and Decius combined. Surely no more archaic document is known in the history of politics. In the first place, ruined temples were to be rebuilt. In the second place, men, women, and children throughout the empire were to come together and sacrifice. Care was to be taken to see that everyone actually tasted the sacrificial victims. In the third place, the market places and the baths were to be consecrated with sacrificial offerings so that every place would have a religious meaning.

This ridiculous decree was answered by Christian volunteer martyrs, most of whom were imprisoned, though many were put to death. In Phrygia a whole town was burned with its inhabitants. In Palestine some Egyptians got into trouble because they were caught by the police while taking food to the prisoners in Cilicia. The governor asked one of them where he came from. He replied that he was from Jerusalem, a city in which only Christians could participate; it lay toward the east and the rising sun. The governor imagined that toward Persia the Christians had established a new city. The Egyptian refused to give any further explanation and was beheaded as an enemy of the state.

By April 26, 311, Galerius had come to realize that his cause was hopeless. The blood of the martyrs, as Tertullian long before had said, was seed. And in his last illness the emperor may have thought that the God of the Christians was punishing him for his bloodshed. Certainly the Christians thought so. He therefore issued an edict of tolerance which brought the long history of persecution, except for minor reactions, to an end. Unfortunately, news of its issue reached Palestine too late to prevent the beheading of Silvanus of Gaza and thirty-nine companions. The edict, issued in the name of all four emperors, reads as follows (we need not give their official titles):

Among other steps which we are always taking for the profit and advantage of the State, we had formerly sought to set all things right according to the ancient laws and public order of the Romans, and further to provide that the Christians too, who had abandoned the way of life of their fathers, should return to sound reason. For the said Christians had somehow become possessed by such obstinacy that, instead of following those institutions of the ancients which perchance their own ancestors had established, they were at their own will and pleasure making laws for themselves and acting upon them and were assembling in different places people of different nationalities.

After we had decreed that they should return to the institutions of the ancients, many were subjected to danger, many too were completely overthrown; and when very many persisted in their determination and we saw that they neither gave worship and due reverence to the gods nor practised the worship of the god of the Christians, considering our most gentle clemency and our immemorial custom by which we are accustomed to grant indulgence to all men—we have thought it right in their case too to extend the speediest indulgence to the effect that they may once more be free to live as Christians and may re-form their churches, always provided that they do nothing contrary to public order. Further, by another letter we shall inform provincial governors what conditions the Christians must observe. Wherefore in accordance with this our indulgence they will be bound to entreat their god for our well-being and for that of the State and for their own, so that on every side the State may be preserved unharmed and that they themselves may live in their homes in security (Baynes).

Galerius was no Christian; the Romans still had their gods; but the right of religious freedom was firmly established, even though under his successors, the Christian emperors, Jews and pagans were to feel the force of Christian oppression.

It had taken Rome many centuries to reach this point. To be sure, earlier emperors had often favored Christianity or had let it alone. The reign of Diocletian and Galerius, however, recapitulates all the religious solutions Rome had tried before and ends with the only possible solution—freedom of religion. The request for prayer which Galerius made of Christians was one with which the Christians had been complying for nearly three hundred years.

Theological writers as well as historians sometimes say that there was an absolute incompatibility between Rome and the Christians and that therefore persecution was inevitable. To say this is to neglect the whole history of Rome's relation to foreign religions and the history of those religions themselves. Early enough it was recognized that the Bacchanalia and the Egyptian religion were not dangerous. At one point they had been dangerous, but as they developed they became allies rather than enemies of the state. Apparently the Roman understanding of Christianity was so limited and so bound up with precedent that simple ignorance was one of the chief causes of persecution. The Romans did not know what Christianity was.

To be sure, the Christians made certain claims for their God which set him above the Roman emperor and the Roman state. But these claims, properly understood, were of the sort which any thoughtful Roman, especially a Roman who valued the Roman Senate, could readily have accepted. There was a double failure of communication. Rome could not express her aims in Christian terms, and Christians could not express their aims in Roman terms. The solution was reached only through the use of the sword against the cross.

We should mention two Christian treatises which were produced toward the end of the struggle. The first, written by a certain Arnobius from Africa, uses all the devices of African rhetoric to ridicule pagan criticism of Christians as responsible for the troubles of the times, and then to make a savage attack on paganism. Arnobius' work reflects the zeal of a recent convert. He seems to know the religions he attacks better than the one he defends. The second, probably composed by the Bithynian rhetorician Lactantius, is a little book *On the Deaths of Persecutors*. It gives a fairly full account of the persecution under Galerius and was written four or five years after Galerius' death. From our standpoint one of its most important features is the sketch of Roman history which its author makes. It shows how one Christian, at least, viewed the struggle through which the church had passed.

Jesus Christ was crucified by the Jews at the end of Tiberius' reign. Then followed twenty-five years of peaceful missionary activity. Under Nero, Peter came to Rome and attracted notice by his miracles; for this reason Nero, a detestable and harmful tyrant, had him crucified and also killed Paul. Nero was punished by not being buried. Some years later another tyrant, Domitian, came to the throne. Demons incited him to persecute the church, and he was punished by the Senate, which condemned his memory and repealed his acts. The church recovered its rights and then enjoyed a very long period of peace, broken only by the "detestable animal" Decius. Like Nero, he was not buried. Not much later, Valerian persecuted the church and was killed ignominiously by Shapur of Persia. Aurelian had planned a persecution but was killed before he could act. Diocletian and Galerius both persecuted the church; Galerius died in agony.

It is obvious that this account is almost entirely erroneous. The Romans, not the Jews, crucified Jesus. No mention is made of the fire at Rome, and the author's idea of the second century is fantastic. On the other hand, he is right in stressing the long years of peace which the church enjoyed, even though he does not understand the legal basis of the intermittent persecutions, or the fundamental attitude of the Roman state toward foreign religions.

III. WHY THE SWORD FAILED

1 The Service of the State

THE ROMAN REPUBLIC AND EMPIRE WERE NOT HELD TOGETHER ENTIRELY by force, and they rested on an ideological structure which the legions defended and extended. No one can doubt the genuine enthusiasm with which provincials, at least in the first two centuries of the empire, were devoted to the emperor and the state. And throughout the history of Rome until the triumph of Christianity the ablest Romans were found in government service.

This ideological structure was closely bound to the old Roman religion as modified under Greek influence, and the twelve gods of Rome were believed to have given Rome her power. To be sure, long periods of philosophical infiltration weakened religious devotion, especially among the upper classes. Varro believed that there was ultimately only one God, worshiped by Romans and Jews alike —though we must remember that his patron, Julius Caesar, counted on Jewish loyalty for his foreign policy. Philosophical monotheism was especially prominent in the second century, but who could doubt that the one god favored Rome? On the other side, with the complete Romanization of foreign religions in the third century, it was obvious that whatever gods there might be served those of Rome. Only disaster could shake the Roman government into awareness that the old Roman gods were dead or dying.

If we want to give a date for the death of the Roman gods, we should perhaps choose A.D. 212 for the boiling point of foreign worships, since their acceptance implied that the old gods alone were inadequate for Rome's needs. Of course, their death agony was long and intense, and we cannot really give any precise year for their demise. Enthusiasm for Vesta and other old Roman deities seems to have increased in the third century, although some emperors treated the Vestal virgins disrespectfully.

On the issue of idolatry the Christians, heirs of Jewish monotheism, believed that they could not compromise. For them there was only one God, the creator of the universe, who stood far above the empire and the emperors. They were convinced that he was the one God because in very recent times he had sent his Son to save the world. The attempts of various Roman officials to work out some compromise could not possibly work, since in the Christians' belief the gods of Rome were demons or deified dead men. The view that they were deified dead men had been held by many Romans during republican times, and the repeated consecrations of good emperors after death obviously implied the truth of this view. Christians, however, regarded the making of gods as idolatry and absolutely refused to participate in it. The worship of the emperor was not forced on them except by Pliny, and Trajan did not approve Pliny's action. But the problem of idolatry remained acute.

As long as the Roman view of the state remained associated with the Roman state religion, the Christian problem could not be solved. The case of the Jews was another matter, for in general the Jews retained their own nationality and their religious rights were protected by treaties dating from republican times. The Christians were an international body. After the destruction of Jerusalem, Jewish missionary activity declined while Christian activity increased. The Jewish problem was settled by the destruction of Jerusalem in 70 and in 135. The Christians had no holy city and no temple on earth. It was impossible to make some kind of concordat with them.

Even the seemingly simple question of a loyalty oath proved insoluble. In the later years of the second century the Christians were asked to swear allegiance by taking an oath by the Genius of the emperor. At this point again, Roman religion was involved. The Genius was the tutelary spirit of the emperor and his family. Christians denied the existence of such tutelary spirits, or regarded them as demons. If the formula was translated into Greek the situation was no better. Genius became "demon" or "fortune" in Greek. The objection to demons was obvious, although Celsus tried to argue for the existence of good demons in his treatise against the Christians. And "fortune" (Tyche) was a goddess widely worshiped in the Roman empire. Clearly Christians could not take such an oath, even though their original opposition to oaths of any kind gradually vanished.

Since these two tests were entirely unacceptable to the Christians, Roman authorities naturally viewed their religion with considerable suspicion. They investigated it, and at the time of the precedent-creating investigation under Trajan they encountered the subversive Apocalypse of John. From this document and from other information in the archives they concluded that Christianity was dangerous and had to be suppressed.

We must now ask a fundamental question. Was it in fact dangerous? Did Christians encourage disloyalty to the state, or were they loyal subjects and citizens of the Roman empire? This question has to be given a historical answer, since Christianity was undergoing changes as it developed from a sect within Judaism to a universal church.

The earliest statement which we have comes from Jesus himself and is found in Mark 12, 14–17. The old Jewish-revolutionary question was asked of him: Shall we pay the census (head) tax or not? This had been the occasion for the revolt of Judas of Galilee at the time Judaea became a Roman province. Jesus replies perhaps by questioning the orthodox Judaism of his opponents; they should not be handling a denarius on which was stamped the image of the Roman emperor. More clearly, he distinguishes two realms: give what is Caesar's to Caesar, what is God's to God. There is a sphere of loyalty which transcends or at least is different from loyalty to the state. But Jesus does not reject loyalty to the state. He insists on double allegiance to Caesar and to God.

The Roman citizen Paul develops the theme of the Christian's loyalty to the state when he writes to Christians at Rome. The Christian must submit entirely to the state which exists (and to its head, who was the emperor Nero). The state has the sword, the power of life and death, in order to maintain order and punish male-factors. The Christian owes it tribute and taxes and obedience. Evidently the apostle cannot conceive of a situation in which the two powers would be opposed, and ultimately he appeals to Rome for a judgment on his life. Similarly, the author of Luke–Acts stresses the legal innocence of Jesus and of his followers and claims that just as Pilate vindicated, or would have liked to vindicate, Jesus, so Roman authorities always acquitted Christians who were brought before them. Writing probably in the reign of Domitian, the author notes the evil nature of royal deification (Acts 12, 21–23), but he does not regard such deification as characteristic of the Roman system. Similarly the author of 1 Peter (compare 1 Tim. 2, 1–2; Tit. 3, 1) urges complete submission to the emperor and the empire (2, 13–17). He is aware that one can suffer "as a Christian" (4, 16), but he knows that sometimes the suffering is due to disobedience of the law (4, 15). He has no clearly developed explanation of Christian suffering but ascribes it to the work of the devil (5, 8). As a loyalist he cannot understand the presence of discord between the two powers. In the gospel of John the early view is reflected: both realms are God's, for while the kingdom of Jesus is "not of this world" (18, 36; compare 19, 12, 15), Pilate's power has been given him "from above" (19, 11). We might suspect that this expression means no more than that Pilate was appointed by higher authority were it not that the evangelist uses such expressions to refer to divine origin. Finally, in Clement of Rome, we find prayer for the empire and the emperors, and an explanation of the persecution under Nero as due to "envy." Clement's enthusiasm for law and order within the church is paralleled by his enthusiasm for law and order in the state.

There is, of course, another strain of thought. Provoked by a crisis in the reign of Domitian which involved the self-deification of the emperor, the apocalyptist John wrote a fiery denunciation of the empire and the emperor in which the question of loyalty does not arise. There can be no loyalty to the Beast or to the Scarlet Woman. The Christian's sole allegiance is to the Jerusalem which is to come. Not only because of its gaudy imagery but also, and specially, be-

cause of its attitude toward the state, the Apocalypse of John proved
an embarrassment to later Christians.

Even though Peter and Paul, and many others, had been killed by
Nero in the year 64; even though a certain Antipas had been killed
(at Pergamum?) in the reign of Domitian; even though Christians
were often endangered, and though Ignatius was to die at Rome: in
spite of these facts most Christians retained their loyalty to the state.

A new difficulty arose in the reign of Trajan when the image of
the emperor was temporarily used as a loyalty test, and under Marcus
Aurelius and his son, when an oath by the emperor's (divine) genius or good fortune was required. The emperor's deity had passed
beyond an honor voted by the Senate to a dead ruler. Such an honor
could be treated as mere formality. The loyalty oath seemed to
imply the actual fusing of Caesar with God; but even at this juncture
1 Peter was written.

The acuteness of the problem resulted in the production of a
whole new body of Christian literature, the writings of the apologists. They believe in the essential justice of the Roman empire in
the second century and find its attitude toward Christians incon-
sistent. They do not "expect a human kingdom but one which is
with God"; they are the empire's allies in the struggle for peace.
They are zealous to pay taxes and they pray for emperors and other
administrators. At the time of the crisis of 176, Melito of Sardis develops the theme of the "mutual recognition and dependence of
Church and State" partly in order to prove the antiquity of Christianity, but primarily because he believes in the positive value of the
empire.

On the other hand, writing in 177 or later, Tatian says that while
the world as a whole is good, its political structure is evil, and he
explicitly says, "I condemn your legislation, for there ought to be
one common government for all; but now there are as many codes of
laws as there are states." Elsewhere he claims that he pays taxes and
serves the emperor, though he cannot obey all the laws.

Tatian's view reflects the circumstances in which he writes. He
admits that "man is to be honored as man" but attacks the legal
formalities accompanying deification, speaks of the emperor as "the

emperor of the Romans," and criticizes the enrollment of convicts in the Roman army. He regards himself as no longer Greek or Roman but barbarian. Similarly a martyr at Scilli in Africa in 180 says, "I do not acknowledge the empire of this age. . . . I pay taxes . . . but my lord is King of kings and Emperor of all nations."

On the other side, Athenagoras says that "we have loyalty and obedience toward you, your house, and your sovereignty" and that "we pray for the emperor and for the succession of his son to the father's kingdom and for the enlargement of his dominions." And a few years later, Theophilus once more stresses honor and prayers for the emperor, who has been given a stewardship from God, though only God can be worshiped.

It is obvious that the martyrdoms of 177 had shaken the loyalty to the empire which Christians professed. The only obligation to Caesar which some Christians continued to recognize was the payment of taxes. They could not remain loyal to an empire and an emperor whose rule was based on patent injustice. These circumstances, more than any psychological problems, explain the violent attack Tertullian makes in his *Apology* of 197. Yet Tertullian himself insists that "we pray for the emperors, for a long life, a secure rule, a safe home, brave armies, a faithful senate, an honest people, a quiet world." Christians pray to God for the emperor, but not to the emperor. The Roman empire will last as long as the world does.

The real problem lay in Rome's confusion of the religious with the secular. Rome claimed that Caesar's realm was based on the power of the gods. Rome could not recognize the existence of areas divorced from the control of the state and its gods, even when faith in the gods had been shaken. The Christian, on the other hand, could not and did not venerate these gods.

Under these circumstances a Roman official might well ask what Christian loyalty actually meant. His own answer to this problem was fairly clear. It had been worked out for him in the last years of the republic, when the upper classes were creating the ideological structure which was to serve the Roman empire. The best citizen, said Cicero, was one who was inoffensive, had pure morals, and was neither subject to passion nor involved in debt. This citizen had created the state which in turn served him. The state rested on a broad base, consisting of

the official religion of worship and divination, executive authority, senatorial influence, statute and customary law, the popular courts and magisterial jurisdiction, good faith, the provinces and the allies, imperial prestige, military and financial strength.

And the state served the citizen primarily by protecting private property. There was to be no invasion of private rights by the state, for it had been created to protect these rights. Only with the recognition of this foundation could both order and freedom be preserved.

Looking back on the reign of Augustus from the early third century, Dio finds these principles unaltered:

He reconciled his authority with the sovereignty of the people, safeguarding their liberty while still preserving security and order; so that the Romans, exempt both from the license of mob-rule and the arrogance of despotism, experienced a sober liberty under the sway of one man but without terror, the subjects of a king but not slaves, the citizens of a democracy without dissension.

That this ideal was most imperfectly realized goes without saying. The crucial problem of the transfer of power from one generation to the next was never solved, although it came close to solution in the early second century. Moreover, there always were peoples within the empire who did not recognize its blessings and were ready to revolt. In the middle of the third century the whole system broke down.

Under good emperors, however, order and freedom were actually achieved to an extent unusual in the history of the world. The good emperors possessed that semi-divine foresight (*providentia*) by which they tried to achieve the permanence (*aeternitas*) of the Roman state. And as we have seen there were many Christians who joined them in praying for the permanence of Rome. The difference between Romans and Christians, as Origen said in his reply to Celsus, was that while Romans looked to the emperor for providential care, the Christians looked to God alone, even though God might well use a good emperor for his purposes.

It is sometimes said that Christians recognized the contingency and temporality of human affairs while Romans did not and that conflict was therefore inevitable. Even the briefest glance through the *Meditations* of Marcus Aurelius will show how absurd such a distinction is. No one could more fully accept the limitations of human existence than he did. Yet he wrote his books while engaged in warfare to preserve the frontiers of the empire. The real difference between him and his opponents is that he was entrusted with the responsibility of government while they shunned it. He had to act; they had only to suffer.

The solution to the problem of the sword and the cross, and the failure of the sword, lies in basic misunderstandings. The Christians were first persecuted because some of them were in fact hostile to the state. We can never prove that there were Christian incendiaries at Rome under Nero, but the mode of their punishment suggests that some were convicted as incendiaries. And in another sense the Apocalypse of John is surely an incendiary book. In the earliest period Christians refused to take oaths of any kind, including oaths of loyalty to the state. Later they came to accept oath-taking but rejected the form which most administrators required. At no time were they willing to offer sacrifices to the Roman gods, but had their leaders been less hostile and more persuasive, it seems likely that some alternative form could have been worked out.

We must go on, therefore, to ask why the Christians, or some Christians, were so hostile toward the state. The answer to this problem lies in the history of early Christian life and thought. The earliest Christians were Galileans, fishermen and others from an obscure area of Palestine. They were Jews who, under the pressure of economic and political chaos, had come to lose all hope of peace and prosperity under Roman rule. When Jesus of Nazareth proclaimed to them that the end of the world was at hand, they took his words literally and followed him in the expectation that God would immediately replace the Roman procurators and the Jewish priests by a ruler of his own choosing. This ruler, they believed, would be Jesus.

When Jesus was not enthroned but crucified they did not lose faith in him. They believed that he was really enthroned at God's

right hand and that he would soon come again to judge the world
and take control over it. This present age was under the control of
Satan, God's adversary; the age to come would be that of the kingdom—or empire—of God. Their enthusiastic waiting for the coming
of God's reign provided the motivation for all their actions. They
could not bring in God's reign and therefore they were not in revolt
against the Roman empire. On the other hand, they would not support and defend the empire against its enemies. They merely gave it
a rather passive acceptance.

Such an attitude was not harmful to the empire as long as the
Christians remained a small sect within Judaism and as long as they
were content to wait. But by the end of the first century it became
evident that Christianity was rapidly growing, and at the same time
it was plain that some Christians were actually hostile to the state.
They were coming to be a state within a state, or as they themselves
expressed it, a "third race of men." Many Christians protested that
they were loyal to the Roman empire, but their ultimate allegiance
was not to the empire. It was to the Christian church and the God
who had brought the Christian church into existence.

The gathering crisis of the empire made it necessary for the state
to proceed more vigorously against subversion, and at the same time
there were some Christians who kept insisting on the idea that the
end was near. No state can tolerate any large body of persons who
proclaim that it is about to come to an end. The rise of Montanism
after 172 has some bearing on the persecutions in the reign of Marcus
Aurelius. Most Christians rejected Montanism, with its claim that the
end was imminent. They did not reject it rapidly or severely enough.

With the rise of Christianity to higher class status by the conversion of Roman citizens, a process which had begun with the apostle
Paul, two things happened. First, Christianity was provided with
apologists of relatively high rank and education, so that it could be
presented in ways intelligible to the Roman government. Their books
inevitably influenced the Christian understanding of Christianity. By
the end of the second century it was no longer possible to view
Christianity as superstition. It had become the philosophical theology
of many members of the aristocracy. Second, Christians of high

rank were able to influence the government and to modify its policy toward the church. This result was beneficial to the church in the early third century, but at a later time, when war was being waged on the upper middle class by the army, it became harmful. Only with the triumph of the middle class could Christianity recover its privileged position.

We can see the process of Christian adjustment going on throughout the second and third centuries, and we shall discuss this process in our next chapter.

2 *The Christian Citizen*

THERE WERE SEVERAL POINTS AT WHICH THE CHRISTIAN WAY OF LIFE could have come into conflict with Roman ideas. We have already seen that the Roman state existed primarily for the protection of private property, and for the combination of authority with freedom on this ground. But private property as such was not the only question involved. Closely related to it were the questions of the status of slaves, for slaves were private property, and the question of military service, for the legions protected the lives and property of Romans. Equally closely related to property was marriage, for through marriage and the family property was protected and transmitted from one generation to another. The Roman wife passed from the authority of her father to the authority of her husband, and the whole process was carefully regulated by an elaborate legal code.

When we consider Christian views we shall see that they are conditioned by the historical circumstances of the church in the empire. The earliest Christians lived in daily expectation of the end of the world, which they both feared and hoped for. In later times this expectation came to fade away, partly because of the passage of time and partly because upper-class Christians had more of a stake in the affairs of this world. This development influenced the whole course of Christian life and thought.

First comes the question of private property as such. Jesus counseled at least some of his followers to sell their possessions and contribute the proceeds to the poor (Mark 10, 21); he told them that they could not serve God and "Mammon," the god of wealth. In the gospel of Luke we find denunciations of the rich which seem authentic, and the same spirit is reflected in the epistle of James. On the other hand, the Roman citizen Paul does not denounce the wealthy, even though he recommends an attitude of aloofness from one's possessions (1 Corinthians 7, 29–30). At this point his ideas are closely paralleled by those of the Roman Stoic Seneca, his contemporary.

In the book of Acts there is a description of primitive church life at Jerusalem which clearly shows that the Christians there practiced a form of communism, even though aspects of voluntary cooperation were preserved. When the end of the world did not come, and when famine struck the Orient between 46 and 48, it was necessary for Christian communities elsewhere to come to the aid of Jerusalem by making "the collection for the saints." Jerusalem communism was apparently unique, and after the decline of Jewish Christianity we hear no more of it. In Paul's churches it was not a regular practice.

In later times the desire for wealth is almost invariably distinguished from wealth itself. Only obscure gnostic sects practised communism, and among them it involved not only sharing wealth but sharing wives. Only somewhat anti-Roman writers like Tatian and Irenaeus criticize private property. Tatian's main objection, however, is to the desire for wealth. And Irenaeus gives an analysis of private property which is close to that of Roman Stoics, especially Cicero. He finally concludes with Jesus that one should make friends with "the Mammon of unrighteousness" (Luke 16, 9) and make use of him for Christian ends. Clement of Alexandria sets the seal of Christian approval on private property. With a significant modification of the earlier question, "Who will be saved?" he asks, "Who is the rich man who will be saved?" His answer is that wealth, and even the pursuit of wealth, is not wrong if the rich man does not give himself over entirely to the pursuit of property but uses it for Christian purposes. And Celsus recognizes that the Christian teaching on this point is not remarkably different from that of Plato. Tertullian is saying nothing new when he insists that the Christian is as devoted to business as the next man. By the end of the second century Christian men of property were actually bulwarks of the state. The real question of the third century was whether the state was a bulwark of private property.

In the second place, there was the question of the status of slaves. In spite of modern romantic notions, it is very hard to believe that Christianity ever attracted many slaves to its beliefs. Throughout the first three centuries Christian writers considered the duties of masters toward slaves and of slaves toward masters in a manner which strongly suggests that they viewed the problem from the masters' viewpoint. We have no letter of Paul to the runaway slave Onesimus; we have only his letter to the slave's master Philemon, urging him to treat Onesimus with every consideration. Modern writers have sometimes thought that Paul suggested that Philemon free his slave, but in view of Paul's plain statement against the use of manumission in 1 Corinthians 7, 21, we may doubt that he recommended anything beyond kind treatment. In this regard the Christian attitude was not in advance of imperial legislation which protected the rights of slaves against cruel masters. The Christian expectation of the end of the world encouraged the freezing of the class structure, and no early Christian writer favors general manumission. In fact, Athenagoras argues that the slaves of Christians do not testify against their masters; this fact proves the masters' moral character. Unfortunately, at Lyons in 177 there were slaves who did so testify. And one of the most unpleasant things Hippolytus could say about his rival Callistus was that he was an ex-slave. At this point there could be no conflict between Christianity and the Roman empire. Though we may recognize that the theory of universal brotherhood in Christ might have led to the ending of slavery, no ancient writer thought of this possibility.

In the third place, the question of military service was solved only gradually. The chief reason for the delay seems to be the fact that Christianity originated within Judaism, and by treaty rights Jews were exempted from military service. Moreover, the teaching of Jesus, with its strong expectation of the end of the world, could easily be interpreted as absolute pacifism. As a Palestinian Jew he could not possibly favor the use of arms against the Romans, and as a Palestinian Jew he could not imagine that his followers would use arms for any other purpose. He taught his disciples that the end would be given by God, not by their own efforts. Those who took the sword would perish by the sword (Matthew 26, 52). The only kind of resistance to the state he envisaged was passive resistance.

New occasions taught new duties, however, and by the time of Marcus Aurelius there were many Roman legionaries who had accepted Christianity. For them it was not a Jewish religion of the oppressed masses. In their view it must have been a religion which had grown up with the Roman empire and contributed to the empire's survival. Melito of Sardis reflects their ideas. On the other hand, these Christians may well have avoided occasions of openly confessing their Christianity. Celsus says to the Christians, "If all men were to do the same as you, there would be nothing to prevent the emperor from being left in utter solitude and desertion, and the forces of the empire would fall into the hands of the wildest and most lawless barbarians." Actually, however, there were many Christians in the army, as both Tertullian and Cyprian testify.

There were of course Christians who expressed disapproval of military service. Tertullian himself attacked it when he became a Montanist, and on the eve of the Decian persecution Origen says that Christians refuse to fight for the empire. The entire accuracy of his statement may be doubted. Christian theologians do not always represent the general conviction of the church. And when both Arnobius and Lactantius seem to reject military service we cannot be sure that their views were widely accepted. In any case, both wrote during the reign of Galerius, and Christians could hardly serve in any army whose functions included their own persecution.

Both Tertullian and Origen came to hold that Christians should not participate in the direct service of the state, whether military or civil. This is to say that they found in love rather than in justice the motivation for their own existence. They stressed the importance of their heavenly citizenship rather than their relation to Rome. Origen even suggested a division of labors. Pagan emperors and their armies ought to fight to defend the empire, while Christians and pagan priests should be exempted so that they could pray. His solution was not accepted either by the church or by the state.

The difficulty with all these attempts seems to lie in the Christian failure to recognize the difficulties of governing a world empire and their rather naïve belief that good will, rather than patriotism, was enough. In part this is related to their common view that the Christian was one who had actually become good rather than evil as a result of his conversion. This perfectionist ideal was not superseded for several centuries. In the second and third centuries they generally believed that all the world's problems would be solved by missionary activity. At this point the Roman emperors, who lacked Christian faith but had some experience of government, were more realistic. In the third century civilians, both Christian and non-Christian, did not recognize the power which the army had actually acquired. It was the task of Diocletian and his successors to restore civil government to its rightful place.

Finally we should discuss the question of marriage, for there were many Christians, especially in the early period, who believed that marriage was a bad thing in view of the impending end of the world. As Paul says (1 Corinthians 7, 9), it was better to marry than to be on fire with passion, but only relatively better. The Apocalypse of John praises those who have remained unmarried (Rev. 14, 4). And popular writings of the second century such as the apocryphal acts were full of admiration of Christian women who left their pagan husbands. The apologist Justin mentions such a case with approval. Obviously such an action would undermine the foundations of society, no matter how much Christian writers might condemn adultery and insist on monogamy. Real approval of marriage is relatively rare, though we find it in Theophilus of Antioch and in Clement of Alexandria. Jesus himself, according to the gospel of Luke (14, 26), had advised his followers to leave their wives.

Tertullian justifies this attitude, as compared with the Jewish family ideal, by claiming that the Old Testament command to "increase and multiply" was relevant in a time when the earth was empty. In the third century, however, it has been filled and overcrowded, and the food supply is inadequate for the number of inhabitants on the earth. Asceticism is to be preferred to marriage. Obviously, with the low productivity of Roman land, his statement was not entirely irrelevant, but a more satisfactory solution might well have been found in greater production rather than in limiting the population.

On the other hand, Callistus, bishop of Rome just after Caracalla's extension of the citizenship, took the step of recognizing marriages between women of high rank and men of the lower orders. Presumably his own slave origin had something to do with his action. But his intention is not unlike that of the state. Other writers at the beginning of the third century insist upon the rightness and importance of marriage; some, though not orthodox, insist on its necessity. By the end of the third century the tension between marriage and celibacy was being solved by differentiating two classes of Christians. The overwhelming majority were to marry and produce offspring.

By the time of the last persecution, then, Christians had come to hold views on the civil duties of man which were in no way opposed to those of the Roman state. This process had been going on for a long time, although occasional outbursts such as those of the apocalyptist John and the heretic Tatian had temporarily set it back. Tatian's prompt condemnation suggests that had the church possessed stronger government in John's time he too could have been rejected. Had it been in the world for a long time it need not have been persecuted under Trajan.

3 Religious Freedom

SINCE IN MANY RESPECTS THE PERSECUTIONS WERE UNNECESSARY, WE still have to ask why they took place. To argue that they simply happened would be to impugn the intelligence and integrity of Christians and Romans alike. Admittedly, as in all human affairs,

there was a certain element of mere happenedness. Perhaps ultimately it was chance that caused the Apocalypse of John to fall into
the hands of the Roman police. At the same time, there is a certain
logic in the appearance of this book at the end of Jewish revolutionary Christianity, and many Christians of the early second century
did not disavow it. We can be sure, however, that had Clement of
Rome known it he would have rejected it without hesitation. But by
the time the majority of Christians could reinterpret it, the time for
reinterpretation was past. On the other hand, we can only condemn
the inertia of Roman officials who did not recognize that Christianity, like the Bacchanalia and the Egyptian religion, had changed
and had in effect become Romanized. Certainly enough Christians
tried to explain this fact to them.

Why did Christianity still seem dangerous? Two facts should be
mentioned at this point. In the first place, Christianity was highly
organized and closely knit. Christian officials were constantly traveling, binding together the brotherhood throughout the world. The
strong episcopal system seems to have developed precisely at the moment when the church was first attacked. The monarchical episcopate
was the creation not only of Ignatius but also of Trajan! Here we see
the empire and facing problems of succession not unlike those of the
empire itself. No other religion except the Roman state religion possessed such highly organized form of government, and unlike the
state religion Christianity was independent of the state.

In the second place, Christianity gradually became articulate as
well as articulated. Toward the end of the second century standards
of orthodoxy were developed and the most brilliant minds the church
possessed began to develop the Christian philosophy. The thought
of Origen is inferior to that of none of his contemporaries except
Plotinus. And Plotinus addressed himself only to those who possessed a technical philosophical education.

In this way Christianity was different from other religions of the
time. Origen spoke in the church's name to all the world.

The theology these writers developed was based on the church's
confession of one God, the creator of all the world, the revelation
of this God in his Son Jesus Christ, and the continued activity of his

Holy Spirit in the church. The church still looked forward to the end of the world and the final resurrection of the dead, but the end was indefinitely postponed. Meanwhile the Christian lived in two worlds, the world of the Roman empire and the world of the Spirit of God. He was a citizen of both. Theoretically the Roman state could have accepted the idea of dual citizenship, but after the time of Caracalla, when Roman citizenship was extended throughout the empire, such a notion was untenable. Moreover, Christians would not perform the symbolic acts required of Romans. We have already explained why they could not do so.

What, then, could Rome have done but carry out its policy of enforced loyalty oaths and sacrifices to the gods? The answer seems to be provided by the course which history actually took. Without denying the reality of the Roman gods (although many Romans did in fact deny it), the Roman government could have offered in 111 the edict of toleration which it finally had to give two centuries later. Doubtless, as Origen says, the total number of martyrs was relatively small, although there must have been several thousand who suffered in the final persecution. Actually, there need not have been any, except for those Christians whose Christianity was a cloak for subversion. It can be argued that by attacking Christians the Roman empire deprived itself of the services of just those men whom it needed most. With Christian aid the crises of the third century might have been averted. And with genuine religious freedom such as was given adherents of other religions (except Manichaeism, which was almost the state religion of Persia), the Christians themselves could have developed their ideas more rapidly and responsibly.

While it is no doubt true that empires inevitably perish, the decline and fall of the Roman empire could probably have been postponed for many centuries had the services of Christians been enlisted in the support of Rome under the God of all, Christians and non-Christians alike. What happened was that after this intense struggle there came an almost equally intense struggle in which Christians became persecutors rather than persecuted. One can hardly blame them. They had not learned tolerance from Rome. Their arguments for religious freedom had been weapons to promote their own triumph, and when their situation was reversed they could not abstain from oppression.

The reason they did not abstain was that the state had failed in its duty to provide authority with freedom and to become a secular agency. The Roman principle that there should be a state religion was responsible for the difficulties of Christians and non-Christians alike. But the state, for its own good, should have refrained from entering into religious conflicts and should have maintained absolute indifference to religious questions. The only duty of the state was to preserve freedom under law, and in performing this duty it failed. It attacked Christianity as subversion and later attacked pagan religion as superstition. Neither of these attacks performed any useful service. Each provided an instance of the state's usurpation of the place of the supreme God, to whom alone belonged the judgment of the various religions of the empire.

For this cause the sword failed. Against the sword the Christians placed the cross, which we can understand as a symbol of their obedience to civil power in matters of the service of the state. They possessed the right, however, to defend themselves against tyrannical interference, for their master had taught them to render to Caesar what rightly belonged to Caesar, while reserving final authority in such matters to God alone.

REFERENCES

The author wishes to express his gratitude to the following presses for permission to make quotations: to the Harvard University Press for the quotation on pp. 15–16 from A. D. Nock, *Harvard Theological Review* 45 (1952), 217; to the Oxford University Press for the quotation on p. 97 from R. Walzer, *Galen on Jews and Christians* (1949), p. 69; and to the Cambridge University Press for the quotation on p. 120 from N. H. Baynes, *Cambridge Ancient History* XII (1939), p. 672.

His principal source of information concerning the various persons named is Pauly-Wissowa-Kroll, *Realencyclopädie der classischen Altertumswissenschaft* (Stuttgart, 1894–   ). Other information, and very full bibliographies, can be derived from the last four volumes of the *Cambridge Ancient History*.

He should mention especially the following works: C. J. Cadoux, *The Early Church and the World* (Edinburgh, 1925); C. N. Cochrane, *Christianity and Classical Culture* (New York, 1944); and H. Grégoire, *Les persécutions dans l'empire romain* (Brussels, 1951).

INDEX